Hug the Monster

Hug the Monster

How to Embrace Your Fears and Live Your Dreams

David Miln Smith, Ph.D.

and

Sandra Leicester

Andrews and McMeel

A Universal Press Syndicate Company

Kansas City

Library of Congress Cataloging-in-Publication Data
Smith, David, 1938 —
Hug the monster : how to embrace your fears and live your
dreams / by David Miln Smith and Sandra Leicester.
    p.   cm.
ISBN 0-8362-1321-1 (hd)
1. Fear. 2. Risk-taking (Psychology) 3. Self-actualization (Psychology)
I. Leicester, Sandra. II. Title.
BF575.F2S59   1996
152.4'6—dc20   95-47466
                                                    CIP

Attention: Schools and Businesses

Andrews and McMeel books are available at quantity discounts
with bulk purchase for educational, business, or sales promotional
use. For information, please write to Special Sales Department,
Andrews and McMeel, 4900 Main Street, Kansas City, Missouri 64112.

To the memory of my father, Seymour, who taught me to observe and to challenge. To the memory of my mother, Gladys, who encouraged me, then crossed her fingers.

To my son, Daren, whose strength, artistic spirit, and knowing smile warm my heart. To my daughter, Chelsea, who inspires me as she boldly challenges practically everything.

And to my partner, Sandy, for her sensitivity and wisdom. Here's to many more dreams coming true together.

—DMS

To my mom, Carol Lester, for her courage, compassion, and sense of beauty.

To my dad, Ernie Lester, for his vigor, enthusiasm, and steady optimism.

And for David, the brightest light I know.

—SJL

Contents

Acknowledgments

Hug the Monster took shape over a period of years and passed through a number of incarnations. We are grateful to John Boswell for listening to our preliminary ideas and for contributing to the early structure of the book. The encouragement of insightful friends helped motivate us, and we owe special thanks to Steven Hoffman, Bob Kriegel, Barbara McNeill, and Susan RoAne, who, at various critical points, said exactly the right things to keep us moving forward.

We wish to thank LeeAnne Brooks, Jonathan Crawford, Carol Lester, Bill Shear, and Bonnie Smith, who read early versions of the manuscript and gave us valuable feedback while cheering wildly. Later, Julia Arno, Violet Cleveland, John Heineman, and Suzy McAllister were generous with their time in helping us refine and improve the content. Extra thanks go to Debra Bentley for reading not one, but several versions of *Hug the Monster*, each time making helpful suggestions, and for supporting us with her love and friendship throughout the entire process. Barbara McNeill unselfishly shared her professional expertise as an editor, and in key spots made some essential improvements. We realize that we're fortunate to have such wonderful, perceptive, and supportive friends.

To Greer Imbrie and staff at Earth House, and Shirley Melnicoe and staff at Northern California Service League, thank you for the years of participation in programs that have not only tested the ideas in *Hug the Monster*, but have yielded some great successes and warm memories. Also,

Wink Franklin's insights and the work of the Institute of Noetic Sciences influenced the spirit of this project in essential ways.

Jean Lowe, our editor, challenged and inspired us throughout the writing process. Thanks to her faith and insight, the stories and exercises blossomed in delightful ways we hadn't anticipated. With skill and gentleness, she demonstrated great care and affection for the manuscript from start to finish. It was our good fortune that she fell in love with *Hug the Monster* at first sight, a synchronous connection we'll always appreciate.

We offer a giant hug and respectful salute to our agent, David Hendin, for believing in us and the book, and for playing an instrumental role in making this dream real. Another thank-you goes to Arlynn Greenbaum for putting us together with him.

Finally, to Lindsay Harrison, who, through her wisdom, wit, and love, directly and indirectly contributed to *Hug the Monster* in dozens of ways, and to whom we are especially grateful for introducing us.

A Note to Our Readers

Hug the Monster" is a playful metaphor that simply means embrace your fears and *go for it*. The title phrase recognizes that personal growth is filled with challenge, that reaching our full potential as humans is a lifelong adventure, and that the best kind of advice involves not mere theory, but actual movement in the direction of self-discovery. Hugging monsters generates excitement. This is a "do-it" book loaded with inspiring true-life stories to get you revved up, and fifty-two exercises to help keep you moving in the direction of your dreams. We enthusiastically argue the case that living our dreams means confronting our fears. Our case is supported with evidence, a few methods, lots of tips, and plenty of fun. Yet, we aren't dispensing advice so much as we are encouraging you to take action and experiment. *The monsters are all metaphors.* As such, they are lighthearted, creative, and arbitrary names we've given to the obstacles we've encountered in our own lives. We wrote from our passion and our life experience while realizing our values may be different from yours. While learning to face change and manage fear is a serious subject, we had plenty of fun inventing and creating the exercises for *Hug the Monster*. We hope some of the spirit of our playfulness shines through, too.

Although a collaborative work, for ease of storytelling, David's voice is identified throughout the book by the pronoun "I." References to "Sandy" refer to the coauthor.

DMS & SJL

Introduction

Hug the monster" is not just a metaphor for me. Over thirty years ago, I started out being an adventurer and athlete who wanted to experience the world. I had no clear intentions of becoming a master of risk taking, let alone the kind of person who would someday write a book called *Hug the Monster* from real personal experience. But that's how things turned out. *Just what do you do when the monsters show up and there's no place to hide . . . ?*

Imagine you are locked up alone in St. Michael's Cave on Gibraltar, where you will spend the night, as I did back in 1972. You've never experienced or even imagined that this kind of darkness could exist—a ghostly underworld of bottomless chambers and endless tunnels where even the sound of your own breathing echoes in ways that suggest you aren't alone. You know that aggressive Barbary apes live on the Rock of Gibraltar, and you can't help but wonder if they live in the cave, too. All you have is a flash light and a head full of stories about people who entered the cave and never returned. . . .

I was in the cave because I had created a series of challenging athletic and psychological events for myself called "Everyman's Olympics, an Adventure Decathlon." It was an Olympic year, and I felt passionately that competition with the self was the highest form of competitive spirit. I wanted to demonstrate the concept by expressing that the Olympic ideals of "swifter, higher, stronger " in body, mind, and spirit are for everyone to emulate, not

just Olympic athletes. The events were tests of psychological as well as physical skill and endurance.

Among the events were swimming around Gibraltar—
something no one had ever done successfully before; taking a blind walk through the labyrinth of alleylike streets in
the old quarter of Tangier; playing the Fool as a storyteller
in the square in Marrakech for dozens of people to observe
and laugh at me; walking on water down the Bouregreg
River using water-walking "shoes"; running a marathon
on the Sahara Desert; climbing the highest mountain in
North Africa; bicycling out of the High Atlas Mountains;
and the fun one—teaching yoga to Danish models in the
exotic gardens of Marrakech. The most difficult event in
my Olympics involved almost no physical skill at all. The
task was simple enough—to spend the night locked in St.
Michael's Cave.

St. Michael's Cave is a tourist attraction during the day,
much like Carlsbad Caverns or Mammoth Cave. A squeaky
steel door locks the cave at night. By special permission of
the government tourist office, I was allowed to spend the
night in the cave, and was even offered a key in case I
changed my mind in the middle of the night. I refused it.

Exhausted from transatlantic jet lag and a strenuous run
through hilly Gibraltar carrying a symbolic torch earlier
that day, I settled into my sleeping bag in a small chamber
inside the cave. The cave came alive with unfamiliar noises
as stalactites dripped and splattered on the sand and rock.
My weary body left me with no mental defenses for the terror that began welling up as I tried to interpret the discon-
certing, eerie sounds coming from below me somewhere
in the pitch-black tomb. Could those really be apes I hear?

I panicked, grabbing for my flashlight, remembering stories of other explorers who'd vanished in the bottomless cave. The flashlight was no comfort, as its beam intercepted and transformed stalactites into a tribe of evil, disfigured, grinning faces that taunted me. My mind raced with fear, my breathing became shallow, and my body turned to rock. I thought my hair was turning white from the terror. I wished I had accepted the key so I could get out of that place. Unsure and disoriented, I was completely unable to move. Logic and objectivity only reinforced the horrifying facts: rock apes, lost explorers, bottomless cave. I was three years old again, facing the fierce, unrelenting monsters of my childhood imagination.

Realizing that my mind was getting me into severe trouble, and that my body, heavy with dread, was of little use to me as a defense, my self-confidence evaporated. I was in a chamber of horrors. Stunned by the fear, I sat motionless, and tried not to breathe; I didn't want to attract attention to myself, nor did I want to be further haunted by the amplified sounds of my own inhaling and exhaling. I lost track of time. Perhaps a full hour had passed when, as if I was witnessing the scene from somewhere outside of myself, it occurred to me to *get above it. I moved my awareness from my head into my heart* . . . and a new feeling welled up and wrapped itself around my fear. Something quite extraordinary shifted inside of me, and a new way of being in the cave presented itself: *"Whatever the monster looks like, I will hug it,* " I decided.

At that moment, I vowed to literally hug the monster when it approached me no matter how hideous, no matter how big, *no matter what*. With that idea as my commitment,

I melted into a sound sleep and survived St. Michael's Cave not only unscathed, but a man rich in spirit for what I had discovered: *fear can literally paralyze, and it can also be overcome.*

The next day I learned that the curator/caretaker of St. Michael's had recently discovered unidentifiable footprints in the cave. To this very day, I still don't know what lurks in the bowels of the cave, or how close I actually came to an encounter with a vicious creature. Yet, my encounter was genuine, and I had made it to the other side of the adventure more alive than ever before.

Years later, upon hearing my report, a highly respected physician and Indian yogi, A.S. Ramchandran, wrote this in an article about my experience:

> To stand back, to take a step back and watch what is happening in the very midst of an intensive activity is given to very, very few and that too only after a long yogic discipline.
>
> David Smith's experience in the cave of St. Michael is of capital importance and gave him a further opening into the greater dimensions of his inner being of the mind and the heart. He had already learnt that his essential physical consciousness can see and do what is necessary without the intervention of his mental thought. This usually spoils the game, he knows, too. In the cave of St. Michael he had the beautiful experience of being in his inner and tranquil mind watching the turmoil of the surface mind and which directed him very correctly to take his station in the heart centre, of a deeper emotion of universal love. This positive force gave him the desired repose.

The lesson repeated itself four years later. In 1976, I decided to go searching for the Loch Ness Monster. While others searched for the legendary monster by boat, I would do it by swimming, actually offering myself as bait. By joining the monster in its own environment, some part of me believed I would find the mysterious creature known to the locals as "Nessie." When the adventure began I was confident I could swim across the loch. I had no fear because I was an endurance swimmer. I chose the place where the creature had been spotted most often, even though it was the widest section of the loch and meant a longer swim. But the loch (Scots for *lake*) is murky and black. Underwater vision is impossible. It didn't take long before I was haunted by mental images of a prehistoric, aggressive, man-eating, swimming dinosaur thirty-five feet in length with a foot-long mouth. I began to get scared.

The lesson of St. Michael's Cave came to me. Could I hug Nessie? Once I answered "yes" to myself—knowing I would hug the monster—I swam in the loch with an exhilarating sense of adventure that gave me courage and determination. I smiled at my former fear. I wondered if Nessie was swimming on its back right below me, just out of sight. Nessie never did show herself to me, but I had the lesson down pat. "When I *think of* a monster, hug it" has been my philosophy ever since.

Risk, like art, is in the eye of the beholder. It is personal. An easy adventure for some is an unappealing, or even frightening prospect for others. We're often shy about confessing our fears. Yet, you can be sure that the things that scare you aren't the same as those of your friends. Our fears are as unique as our fingerprints. They are our special gifts that in many ways determine exactly who we'll become in life. What we push off against—what we avoid and resist—shapes us just as much as the things we love to do. But when you are committed to a life of discovery—both inner and outer—as I have been, eventually you come face to face with the darkness where all monsters lurk.

Within this book are plenty of adventure stories and the lessons I learned from each. I'll tell you about a transforming moment in 1964 when I decided to stop being the aimless guy who smoked, drank, and played around too much as the owner of The Dirty Bird, a bar in San Francisco, and eventually became the first man to swim from Africa to Europe. I'll tell you about kayaking two thousand miles down the Nile, running the Khyber Pass, and trekking the Sahara solo.

But not all of my lessons about fear came from athletic adventures. For example, being a guest on *The Tonight Show with Johnny Carson* ranks right up there with the scariest things I've ever done. Imagine being backstage in the green room with some of the world's superstars and watching them pace, sweat, and even throw up, their fear paralyzing them as they anticipated being next in the famous chair. Being on TV with Johnny might sound like fun, but take it from me, it is totally terrifying.

Over the years, I've developed a method for managing fear, adapting to change, and taking risks. Any monster that has a name can be hugged if you follow the steps I've outlined for you in the pages of this book. They work for me, and for the thousands of people with whom I've shared them.

Since 1988, as a corporate speaker, I have addressed

thousands of business executives sharing my stories and insights about risk taking. Meeting and interacting with so many business people, I see firsthand the consequences of rapid social change, and it is taking a huge toll on people. The loss of job security is a major fear. From the feedback I get, the anxiety over the possibility of losing one's job is almost worse than having already lost it. Clearly, the transition from the industrial age to the information age is disorienting for many of us because the rules are changing faster than we can write them down, and we are unsure of so much.

My definition of pure adventure is *when the outcome is unknown and the unexpected happens.* As such, these times are loaded with adventures, and we need to be better equipped to deal with them. We are living in a new world. To evolve with it, we need new skills to help us manage all the change. Some of the activities we're suggesting in this book may strike you as silly, useless, or mundane. Do them anyway. The payoff is huge. The idea is to learn the five-step method so well that you can integrate it and apply it to your own private monsters. By practicing the exercises and totally harmonizing with the methods they offer, you can use *Hug the Monster* to help navigate the changes, challenges, and adventures in your own life.

Chapter One

Hug the Monster
How to Make Changes in Your Life at Any Age

Fear is that little darkroom where negatives are developed. —Michael Pritchard

Way **to go.** You've decided to learn about hugging monsters, and that's great. We have a lot in common already.

But let me alert you right up front that *reading* and *doing* are not the same thing. This is an action program where fun, excitement, and profound self-discovery are the rewards. No matter what you think about your capabilities right now, the distance between your reach and your grasp isn't all that great once you commit to taking action. Even baby steps count a lot. This is about overcoming obstacles, taking action, and working with the things in life that may be stopping you from living your dreams.

The only equipment you need to get started is an intention to succeed that is just a little bit bigger than your fear of failing. Intentions aren't mere thoughts. They are much bigger and more powerful than ideas. *You can't hug a monster with your head.* Intentions involve your entire being and emanate from your heart. After all, hugging is an act of feeling. Fear often tends to involve the feeling of being all alone. The dynamic of a hug involves connecting. This is the secret to the whole thing. The exercises, when done from the heart, will teach you about yourself and how much more you are capable of in all of the areas of your life.

How fast are things changing in the world? "You can't

step into the same river twice," observed Heracleitus in describing the essential nature of our lives and the continual
ebb and flow of change. I wonder what he would have said
if he'd lived in the contemporary United States instead of
Greece around 500 B.C. Perhaps he would have been among
the first to speed up the on ramp of the information super-
highway and order a pizza on the Internet. Or perhaps not.

So Many Monsters . . . So Little Time

These are high-speed times, and they require ways of
living and relating that even the wisest philosopher could
never have imagined. Technology may be making us
smarter intellectually, but who among us would declare
that we are happier and healthier? Social indicators of
lifestyle and disease suggest that feelings of fragmentation,
isolation, loss of control, and conflict are on the rise even
though we are better educated and are enjoying more material comfort than ever before. *What's going on here?*

We can't become what we are destined to be by remaining who and what we are. This is both the challenge of evolution, and the paradox of change. Learning to manage
change suggests mastering ourselves in the process. Indi-
vidually and collectively, perhaps our greater destinies will
be shaped by our ability to make healthy, courageous, and
wise choices. All work, as it turns out, is personal work.
The quality of awareness that we bring to our daily lives is
far more important than we ever knew. Or as business
management guru Peter Drucker says, "Defending yesterday is far riskier than making tomorrow." But exactly who
are we becoming, and what kind of tomorrow are we making?

How to Use This Book

We've tried to make this book as interactive and user friendly as possible. You may want to use a notebook and declare it your *Hug the Monster* journal for making notes, jotting down ideas and insights as they come to you, for planning your adventures. Record names, dates, goals, fears, and even phone numbers.

The exercises are organized to match the ways we tend to approach our lives—in categories. Maybe we think we're good at logic and weak at creativity. Or perhaps our professional lives are going great, while our relationships at home need help. We might think we're more artistic than we are athletic. We tend to frame our life experiences based upon our core identities, or who we believe ourselves to be. Hugging monsters expands and enlarges the self. You'll find exercises in six broad categories: for essential self-awareness, for boredom, for stimulating creativity, for relating to other people more easily and openly, for going on some bigger adventures, and for reframing some of the fundamental questions we ask about the meaning and purpose of our lives. The greatest adventure of all—the chance to discover what it means to be fully human—is available to us every moment of our lives. Helen Keller knew this when she said, "Avoiding danger is no safer in the long run than outright exposure. Life is either a daring adventure or it is nothing." Adventure involves the unexpected, the unknown, and the untried. Monsters come with the territory no matter who you are.

We also suggest that using the buddy system will speed your progress and add depth to your experiences. Ask a good friend or partner to join you in your *Hug the Monster* program, and keep track of one another's work. Share your dreams, fears, and goals with each other. Making changes in our lives is always easier when there's someone close by who can support us, especially when it comes to breaking patterns.

By the time you get to the end of the book, especially if you do all of the activities we suggest, you may begin to understand that categories themselves are illusions. One possible insight is the realization that the same patterns and processes are operating inside us no matter what activity we are engaged in. Monster hugging means accepting the present moment for *what it is*, and going from there. The point of power is always to be found in the present moment. Finding the present moment is easier when the ego relaxes its grip, stops insisting on being right, and allows learning to take place. In the words of golf great Jack Nicklaus, "Maybe I'll play well today, maybe I'll win. Maybe I won't play well, and won't win. But whatever happens, I'll learn something from it."

What is the best way to approach these exercises? If you believe you are good at something, you are more likely to take a risk, right? In other words, you are willing to challenge yourself in an area where your self-confidence is already established. That's great. In that case, you may want to begin with the exercises that seem the easiest. But why limit yourself? In *Hug the Monster*, we're going after something different. In addition to expanding your comfort zones for greater successes, this is about going for the things you aren't that good at. The idea behind *Hug the Monster* is that the benefits of making a sincere effort show up in surprising places. That not being a couch potato any longer may actually get you a promotion at work. That taking up running, or some other form of physical activity, may stimulate your artistic side. That becoming more open with strangers may result in a new ability to enjoy solitude and meditation. Sound intriguing? Let me explain.

What Happens When You Hug a Monster?

My career as an adventurer began unexpectedly one summer evening in 1964. I was with my girlfriend standing on the Golden Gate Bridge, complaining about the lack of direction in my life, about drinking and smoking too much, and about generally not respecting the choices I had made to that point in my life. I had no worthy goals. I had plenty of money, nice clothes, two fast cars, and a country club membership. My life looked great on the outside, but it didn't feel good on the inside. When my girlfriend asked me what I wanted to do, I offhandedly mentioned to her that I'd always wanted to swim the Golden Gate.

Her response caught me off guard. "Then why don't you do it?" she said. I repeated, "No, I always *wanted* to do it," clarifying that I was talking about a faraway desire, not an immediate intention. But with her question, something started to shift inside of me. It was below my conscious level of thought, as I had no particular framework or skills to recognize it as a breakthrough moment. But it was definitely accompanied by a certain amount of dread. Swimming the Gate would mean shifting my very identity from someone who had a dream, to someone who had a tangible goal.

My girlfriend encouraged me by telling me she believed I could do it if I made my mind up to do it. The old me grew very still inside, and the possible me stirred. It was the same familiar voice inside, but it was more animated, more alive. It was a turning point for me.

I decided to believe that she was right. I announced my

new goal to friends and regular customers in my bar, and they all laughed. "Sure you are," they mocked. They immediately started placing bets against me. These were the people who saw me partying every night. They knew what it would take, perhaps even more than I did at the time. It was a real stretch. I was totally out of shape. My high school swimming days were ancient history. The first time I got in the swimming pool I was humiliated to discover I could swim only two laps. But it was a start. I adjusted my expectations and increased my distance each time I swam.

Within a surprisingly short period of time, those two laps became ten, then twenty, and then fifty. Before long, I was ready to train in the chilly waters of San Francisco Bay, and I joined a group of experienced Bay swimmers called the Dolphin Club, where I found new camaraderie and support. Months later, on October 17, 1964, my twenty-sixth birthday, I successfully swam "the Gate," opening up to me a life I hadn't even imagined was possible. The monster seemed huge. Yet all it took to hug it was practice, support, and a little determination to stretch, to swim two more laps than I had done the day before.

Cross Training as a Useful Metaphor

The strategy of cross training is practiced by many athletes, and I believe it has a few applications in monster hugging, too. The idea in cross training is to add variety and stimulation as you expand, balance, and heighten awareness in the mind-body by practicing multiple sports even if you want to specialize in a single sport. As a triathlete for many years, I can attest to the benefits of combining running and bicycling with swimming, for example. Increased flexibility and added strength and endurance are just a few of the benefits.

It is unlikely that you'll find any activity in your life that doesn't spill over into other areas of your life. This idea is summed up beautifully in a workbook titled, *How You Do Anything Is How You Do Everything* by Cheri Huber. If you are afraid of self-disclosure and intimacy at home, chances are this same personality trait is operating at the office where you may tend to remain aloof, preventing you from enjoying the excitement and joy that real teamwork generates. If you are willing to put yourself on the line in an area you normally avoid, such as dancing, the mere act of taking dance lessons may contribute to a greater sense of well-being that shines a light into previously hidden corners of your personality.

Because *Hug the Monster* exercises get at core issues, the positive benefits will spill over into all areas of your life if you will let them. You don't necessarily need to declare you are after a wholesale shift in your attitude about life. Just do the exercises and watch it happen.

How Many Kinds of Monsters Are There?

I'm not a trained psychologist, and for the most part my expertise comes from life experience, not textbooks. While there are millions of possible monsters, for our purposes there are three basic kinds of fear. The first is an instinctive, alarmlike response to a genuine, life-threatening circumstance. If you've survived a natural disaster, a house fire, or car crash, or live and work in a high-crime area, you may know this type of fear. The second and far more common fear is the sort that involves change and the unknown. The third kind is specifically associated with phobias such as fear of heights, snakes, or crowded spaces. Personal belief systems, experiences, and habits—unconscious responses to events—can be powerful tools, or they can be monsters, depending upon the effects they deliver consistently. Let me explain.

In the first few days of kayaking on the Nile, almost everything looked like a crocodile to me. Logs floating in the river and shadows cast by debris along the river's edge all suggested fear and danger. Before I learned to recognize crocodiles for real, my imagination conjured them up where they didn't exist. I had to become a student of the river and the environment before my adrenaline could fall back to reasonable levels.

Our experience has everything to do with our beliefs. If you work in a zoo feeding and caring for reptiles, your response to seeing a real snake will be different than if you are someone who, having very little experience, is paralyzed at the sight of one. Phobias are not exempt from being overcome using the five-step method that is explained in detail later in this chapter, but some phobias may not be successfully overcome through cross training, requiring concentrated work instead.

While you may not be able to change external events happening in your life right now, you can learn to change your response to them. This isn't a dissertation on the psychological and physiological aspects of fear. It is an action book about working with certain kinds of fears—fears that come from swimming in the currents of change and the unknown. These changes mean that you must risk challenging the status quo of your life—the status quo is actually our primary target.

In chapter 2, the warm-up exercises ask you to take a closer look at your dreams, fears, and values. Are you haunted by broken promises to yourself? Are you serious about your dreams, or do you just talk a good game? And what about your fears, anyway? Can you name them?

Having dreams and fears is certainly part of life, but if you've stuffed them into an invisible black bag and only haul them out on New Year's Eve when it's time for making resolutions again, there's probably more anxiety than hope and joy in the ritual. Even all of that is okay. The slate can be clean anytime you say it is. You'll be asked to honestly evaluate your relationship to your dreams, fears, strengths, weaknesses, time, values, and money. To find out how well you know yourself today, just imagine removing money as an obstacle to living the life of your dreams. Dig deep. Notice all the if's and but's. Are the limits real? This is the adventure of *Hug the Monster* warm-up exercises. Make lots of notes.

Do the warm-up exercises bravely and honestly and a treasure map to your true self may emerge, becoming the basis for how you approach the other exercises where the kind of action you take is an answer to the perennial question, "Who am I?" The late J. Krishnamurti was an Indian philosopher whose teachings help millions of people, including myself, gain greater self-knowledge. "Truth is a pathless land," he said. In other words, if you find yourself on a particular path invented and drawn by someone else, it isn't *your* path. Hugging monsters is my own interpretation of this idea. No one else has monsters exactly like yours, so how and when you choose to hug them is totally up to you.

The Five Stages of Getting to Know Your Monster

As a lifetime adventurer, I don't go looking for trouble or empty thrills, and I don't take fear lightly. It isn't very helpful to have some well-meaning friend say "It's all in your head" when your stomach is in knots, your sweaty palms are dripping like a faucet, and you feel like you could pass out or throw up from the thought of doing what scares you. You need to learn about your monsters before you can hug them.

Fear comes up when we face the unknown, generating a feeling that we aren't adequately prepared. In my own experience, I have found that when we take the time and effort to prepare ourselves, we discover adequate supplies of courage and confidence. In his essay "Courage," Ralph Waldo Emerson wrote, "He has not learned the lesson of life who does not every day surmount a fear." He speaks of courage as "equality to the problem before us." I also like Winston Churchill's belief that courage is "the most important of virtues because it is what they all depend upon." If we don't prepare, fear is nature's way of letting us know we have some work to do. Perhaps it is our signal that change is in order. I do not advocate pushing through fear with machismo or false bravery. If you want to achieve the goal or dream enough, you'll take the time to prepare.

A wiser part of me refuses to oversimplify the adventures I decide to go after. I have learned to make sure I understand the nature and the magnitude of things that I do. As a result, over the years of adventuring and taking risks, along with my fair share of misadventures, I've developed a five-step method that keeps me focused on the essentials—things that I might otherwise overlook out of eagerness for the thrill, enthusiasm to get going, or sheer expedience. Perhaps you have your own method, and if it works for you, keep using it. Having patience to do things the right way is one expression of your commitment to success. Every exercise in this book is based upon a five-step approach. It will help place your emphasis on *taking the time* to accomplish your goal. Memorize it right now. It will practically guarantee your success. When considering any monster, here's what you do.

1. Gather information.

Fear and darkness go together, and so do information and light. Fear comes from ignorance. It is generated as a result of what we don't know. To end ignorance, we must get more information. *All kinds of information. As much as possible.* Having awareness of what we don't know is like flicking on the light switch in our minds. Try cleaning and tidying up a room in the dark with the lights out. It can't be done. The first step in my five-step method is the equivalent of flipping the switch, beaming floodlights in your monster's face.

A beginner's mind is a great thing to cultivate. It means you have tossed out any preconceived notions, good or bad, and that you intend to become a learner. Hopefully, you'll be a lifelong learner. In any case, you have things to learn about your monsters, otherwise they wouldn't even *be* monsters.

I grew up on *National Geographic* magazine. When I became an adult, I knew exactly how to feed my sense of adventure. When I decided I wanted to run in East Africa where First Man ran and hunted, I started learning everything I could about the environment, the people, the language, and the specific skills I would have to master. From watching films and videos, I saw re-creations of how the early hunters moved and what they sounded like. I studied maps, looked at the environment from the points of view of the bush animals, and talked to people who had been there. Doing the research is often its own adventure, and filled with fun.

Every challenge begins with thorough research. The object is to work with facts, and not beliefs, hearsay, or even experience. For example, if you have vowed to finally lose those twenty-five pounds, you don't just begin a diet. You learn about your body and the nutrition it needs. You read. You talk to people who've lost twenty-five pounds and kept them off. You see your doctor. You learn about fat grams, how to burn calories, and how long it will reasonably take you to achieve your goal based on your body type and metabolic rate.

Gathering information often occurs on multiple levels. Once you've spoken with your doctor, learned about fat grams, and established an eating routine, you'll *assess* the facts you've collected, and your *strategy* may be to add an exercise program to accelerate your body's metabolism. In the process you may experiment with the kind of exercise that works best for you. A walking program may be just right at first. Later, you may add bicycling, jogging, low-impact aerobics, or in-line skating. Or you begin by walking two miles every Monday, Wednesday, and Friday, and work up to three miles five days a week. Adjusting your course as you go along suggests that *flexibility* is also an essential part of information gathering. Learn to be flexible, keeping your sights fixed on the long-term goal while adjusting your interim activities.

2. Develop the skill—do your two laps.

As the proverbial saying goes, "Inch by inch it's a cinch, yard by yard it's hard." Practice and rehearsal develops your skill, which in turn leads you to your goal. But that's not all it does. It is often essential to your health and safety, as well. Which reminds me of one of my own experiences . . .

In 1960, I was in Pamplona, Spain, to experience the world-famous annual weeklong festival of the running of the bulls. Like many Americans, I had read and loved Hemingway's *The Sun Also Rises*, which popularized Pamplona, and I was fascinated by the entire spectacle as a participant. Every morning at six A.M., the bulls were released from a pen and charged through the narrow streets some five hundred yards into the arena. Crowds of people watched from windows and rooftops as several hundred thrill-seekers, myself among them, sprinted with the bulls into the ring. Each afternoon I attended the bullfights. Especially inspired by the artistry and grace of matadors, I decided I wanted to have the experience of being a matador, too.

I read books about matadors and their techniques, learning about different passes with the cape and muleta. I had already seen all the films ever made on the subject. I studied with a young matador for a few hours one afternoon. Being such a longtime fan of the sport, I thought this was all the preparation I needed. Like a madman, I entered a small ring with a small, five-hundred-pound bull—without a cape. Contrary to the popular notion, it isn't the color red that bulls react to, it is motion that invites their charge. The young bull headed straight for me at full speed.

Facing the charging bull, I remembered a move I saw a matador make several years before and attempted to repeat it. It played like a movie in my mind's eye: I would extend my right leg to the side, presenting a target for the bull. The bull would make the adjustment to my new position, and just as he was about to gore, I would shift back to my left foot as the bull passed by. I felt a split second of pride for knowing what to do. Yet, not surprisingly, the theory didn't hold. I wasn't quick or skilled enough. Instead, the bull sent me flying through the air, landing me first on the ground, and in the hospital immediately thereafter.

Whatever monsters you choose to hug, I hope you'll learn from my misadventure in the bullring, and always remember that research alone isn't enough. It's a good idea to keep your pride in check so you'll never enter the ring with underdeveloped skills.

As you develop your skills, realize that small steps eventually give way to quantum leaps in your ability to hug monsters. Skill development always has a starting point. You must *find your two laps* and begin. *Self-discipline*, a requirement of skill development, is much easier to attain once you realize that practice, rehearsal, and experimentation can be fun. A visual image that illustrates this point is a well-worn path in a field. The path has been walked many times, and the grass is matted down. When we hug the monster and change our path, the grass will be very tall at first and the direction we are heading will not be very clear. But by continual practice—two laps at a time, so to speak—we will eventually wear a path that we know. We will have blazed a new trail. Likewise, when you first learned to ride a bicycle, chances are your learning curve included falling off the bike. That's not failure, that's part of the process. If you can learn to look at *failure* in a new way—as essential *feedback*—you'll have a lot more fun, and learn a lot faster, too. For example, when I'm working on a new speech, I schedule talks with local service clubs in my community where the stakes aren't too high, where I can enjoy meeting new people and hear valuable feedback on my new program. The feedback nearly always improves my program.

3. Set the date.

Sometimes I do this step first—setting the date in order to force the rest of the steps in the plan. "I am going to the

Amazon for six weeks next December 10" is a statement you make nine months or even two years earlier, and then do the other steps with that date in mind. But that's not all. You make the airplane reservation, or better yet, buy the ticket. Make sure you take enough time, and that the date is realistic. You must be firm about it, allowing nothing to get in the way. I've done this dozens of times, and it works like a charm, attracting the information, resources, energy, and resolve to make the dream a reality.

You declare your intentions on a calendar, and tell three other people. Paste up the date around the house if you want to—a note on the refrigerator, a memo to yourself on the bathroom mirror. Make it real. You've always wanted to be able to play Beethoven's *Moonlight* Sonata on the piano? Don't merely start taking lessons. Schedule a performance and tell six friends to be at your house on May 19, even though today is only November 10.

Always wanted to skydive? Now there's a monster plenty of people would love to hug. These days it is easier than you think. Beginning skydivers can jump in tandem with an experienced jumper. You don't have to do a thing other than attend ground school and then get in the plane. Knowing this, what is most likely to stop you? Not taking the time and setting the date.

4. Don't think about it, just hug it.

I used to love watching live space launches from Cape Canaveral on TV. I always held my breath as the countdown went from ten, nine, eight, seven, six . . . to liftoff. I didn't realize that the countdown had been going on at NASA for months, and that I was only hearing the final ten seconds of literally years of work. Hugging monsters is like that. Hug It Day always comes. You can *count* on it.

With information gathered and the skill developed, now *you* are ready for liftoff. Suspend judgments and you won't be stopped, especially if you keep your commitment to doing your very best, no matter what. If you've followed the method so far, you are in control because you've minimized the downside by capitalizing on all of your strengths. When the day comes, nothing is more important than hugging the monster. If you're like me, you're bound to feel excitement. You'll no doubt be a little bit nervous, too. And why not? You've invested your ego, your time, perhaps even some expense. I don't often use the word *luck*, because it implies a minimum of participation in our own lives. We have to be responsible for our actions and their consequences. Yet, adventure involves the unexpected. To that end, if the best definition of *luck* is "preparation meeting opportunity," then you can expect plenty of good fortune on Hug It Day when you've followed the steps in this method. You've researched your mission. You've rehearsed and practiced. *You can do it*.

5. *Reflect*.

Have you ever noticed that growth isn't always obvious at the time it is happening? Humans are endowed with a marvelous capacity to reflect. Once you've accomplished your goal, take time to relive all of the steps and the feelings you felt along the way. An essential part of reflection is establishing internal points of reference—that is, three-dimensional memories of how it felt to hug the monster. Use your inner senses to hear, see, smell, taste, touch, and feel all that went on during the event. Replay it like a mental movie, reinforcing the memory. Notice what stands out the most. Learn from the experience, commit it to memory from beginning to end.

I love to remember and reflect. I can still recall how it felt to swim the Golden Gate the first time—physically and emotionally. The memory remains loaded with good energy that I often put to new use. And I can still feel the scorching sun on my back during the first few weeks of my two-thousand-mile kayak journey down the Nile, my skin turning deeper shades of brown with every passing day. I smile remembering the Nubian crocodile hunters eyeing me and my kayak suspiciously, only to later invite me to have lunch with them.

Memories such as these are points of reference that will create the cross-training effect of expanded, heightened, balanced awareness. They will show up again and again in future monster-hugging adventures to remind you of past successes and to provide confidence and solid proof that you are capable of almost anything.

Another part of reflection is in telling your story to others. As Muriel Rukeyser said, "The universe is made of stories, not atoms." In the retelling of an event, you make vital connections with yourself and with others.

When I swam from Africa to Europe the first time, I started out believing it was a solo adventure, a difficult feat involving me against the impossible currents. Everyone knew it was impossible. The odds of success were against me, and the obstacles were huge. No one had ever done it before, although plenty had tried. I swam behind a fishing boat that pulled a large, flimsy cage that in theory was supposed to protect me from sharks. Two hours into the swim, I was sick to my stomach from drinking the salt water that sloshed into the gulps of pure Coca-Cola syrup I drank for energy.

I began to fear that the pain would grow worse and that I wouldn't reach the shore. Hours later, the muscles in my shoulders and groin felt like hot pokers were jabbing them with every stroke. Nothing in my experience could have prepared me for the chest pains that tortured me—the result of swimming while having dry heaves.

With each labored stroke, I rationalized that I just couldn't handle the physical pain. No one had ever succeeded at this, why should I? My mind called up all the possible reasons for how and why I could give up and not look bad. One option was especially seductive. I could merely concede, "They were right. It is impossible. I've proven it." But I also knew I wasn't there to rationalize. I was there to connect two continents—to swim from Africa to Europe.

At the lowest, most awful point of the swim, I looked up at the people on the boat in front of me. It was clear they were sharing my pain. Some of them were sick, too, throwing up off the side of the boat. They each had invested their own time and resources for this swim. Their faces were so full of determination. They needed this victory as much as I did. In that glance, I knew that I had to do my part. I realized that my success was as important to them as it was to me. We were all in it together. It was a very emotional moment, and I cried in my goggles. Out of it all, I found new strength, stamina, and determination, words I repeated like a mantra with every stroke. In what seemed like only moments later, there I was staggering onto the shore, hearing Horace Zammit, my greatest champion and ally, say, "Congratulations, David. You are the first bloke to do it!" Bernard, the wise old fisherman who piloted our boat, had seen others attempt the torturous swim and fail. He was fond of telling people I accomplished it with my heart and not my lungs. Perhaps he saw the connection I would later understand more fully.

From reflection comes growth. It wasn't only my victory.

We were a team. It was *our* victory. None of it would have been possible without the assistance of dozens of other people—those who helped me train and those who hung in there for the whole thing. That golden insight was an unanticipated bonus of swimming from Africa to Europe, and it serves as an important reminder to this day. By reflecting on this experience, I learned about team building, something I might have missed if I wasn't committed to a program of reflection. Now and then, the monsters hug you back, rewarding you with far more than you could ever reasonably expect. (Horace later became the mayor of Gibraltar, largely due to the recognition he earned by helping spearhead the effort and gather the resources that were needed for our success.)

Exactly What Is a Monster?

A monster is anything that seems to stand between you and your happiness, peace of mind, and/or sense of well-being. We say *seems to* for a good reason. Here's why. As long as you choose not to hug the monster, it indeed stands firmly planted between you and whatever your goal is. It may even bring on anxiety, sleepless nights, guilt, shame, or *any other kind of negative feeling that is a consequence of being in conflict with yourself.* As long as you avoid your monsters, you may feel trapped and controlled by them.

Yet the moment you approach the monster directly, it transforms into a kind of energy force that actually propels you toward your goal. With each monster you hug, use the five-step method we've suggested and you'll experience joyful feelings of freedom, self-confidence, and happiness knowing you really are in control of your own life. Success breeds success. The more monsters you hug, the better you get at it. Once you learn to recognize inner conflict for what it is—a valuable opportunity to grow and experience something wonderful—you probably won't hesitate to make monster hugging a way of life.

Bonus: When the Monster Hugs You Back

Before you start doing the exercises, I will share one last insight that my monsters have taught me over the years. Perhaps it is the most important thing to know about getting ready to do the things that frighten and threaten us.

When you begin an exercise, chances are you already have the ideal outcome in mind. You can picture what success looks like, and to some degree, the result is fairly predictable, so far as the action itself is concerned. If you are afraid of public speaking and you agree to begin a program to hug that particular monster, success comes in the form of taking the action and giving the speech to an audience. You feel terrific because you accomplished something difficult. But it may not end there.

Sometimes there's an unanticipated bonus. We call this "when the monster hugs back." Synchronicities tend to show up when we are "in synch" with ourselves and our environment. *Being in synch is the exact opposite of being in conflict.* For example: when you give your speech, in the audience may be your new best friend, or someone who wants to hire you for the job of your dreams. Perhaps giving a speech will change your entire life, just like swimming two laps did for mine. I don't mean to imply that this will happen all of the time, but I want to alert you to the possibility. When the monster is bigger than life, a life-size amount of energy is involved in the hug, too. When that energy is released, the results often include pleasant, even amazing surprises.

The art and skill of monster hugging involves adequate preparation. Small victories lead to bigger ones, and every goal you set and reach counts. However, for the biggest payoff of all, make sure you are living your own dreams. We can trick ourselves for months, years, even decades, believing we're living according to our true values. Only eventually do we realize that our lives are not authentic at all, but rather lived according to someone else's rules, out of a larger, unnamed fear. Self-knowledge comes from life experience, an open mind and heart, and learning to recognize our monsters for what they are—voices deep inside us that are asking to be heard.

Be in the Monster-Hugging Hall of Fame

I collect stories of other people's successes. Few things mean more to me than being a witness to another's victory. I often take people on outdoor adventures. When fifty-five-year-old Richard, a banker, leaned back to rest on the side of the mountain during his first-ever rappelling experience, I shouted down to him, "Are you okay?" concerned he might be having a crisis of some kind. He looked up at me and grinned. Finally, he spoke. "I've wanted to do this all my life. I'm going to savor every moment of it." Life just doesn't get any better than that. Richard's in my personal hall of fame for the most wonderful and uncharacteristic "I did it!" shout when he reached the ground.

And there are the life-changing monsters. I met and became friends with Sandra Leicester, coauthor of *Hug the Monster*, at a time of radical change in her life. When, at thirty-five, she realized her ten-year marriage was over, she began asking herself, "if I could have the ideal life for myself, what would it look like?" In the face of that question, her success as the owner of a small advertising agency in Indianapolis wasn't enough. So she started to dream bigger dreams. She imagined herself as an author, writing books while living in a place near mountains and an ocean, and connecting with the people whose work in mind-body health and healing she was fascinated by. Quietly, she did a little research. Then, on a dare to herself, she took a long shot and made an inquiry to such an organization in the Bay Area, offering herself as a marketing consultant. To her surprise, they said yes.

Nine months later, with very little savings and a six-month consulting contract, she said good-bye to her family and lifelong friends. She moved to San Francisco, where she knew absolutely no one, and began building a new life. I was her first new friend. She was soon meeting and working with many of the people whom she had long respected and admired. I watched and offered support through a remarkable transformation that included changing her name, her physical appearance, and her lifestyle. She hugged dozens of monsters. In those early weeks and months, we talked a lot about taking risks. The idea for a book called *Hug the Monster* came out of all those discussions. That was over six years ago, and we've been a great team ever since.

No matter what you think about yourself today, you are capable of much more. We all are. What labels do you wear? Executive. Wife. Friend. Son. Plumber. Musician. To the extent they define you, these are limits. You are more than your body. More than your personality. More than your job, house, bank account, and lifestyle. *You are spirit*

expressing what you know on the way to becoming even more.
We're all growing, changing, moving in directions that call
to us from a deep, unknown place inside. Most of us go
through life either failing to recognize or ignoring the voice
that calls us from deep within. This book is about learning
to recognize, listen, and respond to that voice with an
eager, open heart. It is about identifying what the voice is
telling us about the fears that hold us back, and taking action toward positive changes. Thank goodness we're living
at a time when inner exploration is understood to be an important aspect of our growth and development as humans,
and perhaps no longer perceived as a self-indulgent activ
ity as it once was. These days, we have many more resources than even a decade ago, and using them, we can
more easily encourage ourselves and each other to ask
questions and investigate ways of being in the world together that promote health and well-being.

We live in a world where instant gratification is available to each of us all of the time. Credit cards, automobiles,
airplanes, shopping malls, telephones, computers, and especially the remote control for the television mean we can
alter our external experience instantly. While I'm not complaining about the ease of modern living, I also know that
all of this instant convenience is robbing many people of
the ability to find out who they really are inside. Discovering inner strength is ultimately one of the greatest, most
satisfying things in life. When you have it, no other reward
is necessary. Unmistakable waves of clarity, insight, generosity, and joy accompany the discovery of inner strength.
It makes people glow inside and out. I want to live in a
world full of people who glow. Don't you?

Some say it is the destination that counts. Others say it is the journey. I say it is both. And whatever the "it" is, you can be sure it will be bigger, better, and more joyful than your ability to imagine it.

My one-word philosophy on life is: *"Yes."* How about you? What is the greatest risk you've ever taken in your life? Can you imagine not having taken it? Probably not. Conversely, what risk do you feel some regret for not taking? What would your life be like today had you found the skills, courage, and support to say yes instead of no?

Our lives go by in a flash. We aren't given any guarantees. Daily we are given the opportunity to face the facts of our existence and the very nature of our lives: *Nothing remains the same, and nothing lasts forever.* Monsters are the gifts we give ourselves—in gigantic proportion they bring to our lives confidence, satisfaction, and positive challenges *to be more.* Hugging them is an affirmation of life and an act of profound self-love. They stand like sentries at the gates of sacred ground—the landscape of our lives. When we view our monsters in a new light, we see that they are constant reminders that we really have nothing to lose and everything to gain. Our monsters can keep us excited about life. And in the end, what else is there?

You've done it before, and you can do it again. Say yes. Hug the monster.

Chapter Two

Warming Up to Our Monsters

*Set me a task in which I can put something
of myself, and it is a task no longer; it is
a joy; it is art.*   —Bliss Carmen

This chapter contains seven warm-up exercises to help
you feel as prepared as possible for the monsters you'll be
hugging in the weeks and months to come. Hopefully, the
warm-ups will reveal some essential self-knowledge and
lay some foundations for the work, adventure, and fun
ahead. Consider taking yourself on a mini-retreat—either
at home or in some other special place. Plan ahead to set
the time aside. Pack a picnic lunch and head to your favorite park. Or spend an entire afternoon in a cozy café. Or
let your answering machine take your phone calls, light a
fire in the fireplace, load your CD or tape player with your
favorite quiet music, and announce to those who live with
you that you don't want to be disturbed for several hours.

A major theme in *Hug the Monster* is that we learn and
grow best by doing, rather than just thinking. The previous chapter offered you the five-point method for How to
Hug a Monster. To help you learn the method, in this chapter we ask you to apply it to an event in your past—one in
which you took a risk successfully. You may discover that
the method is organic—that you've followed it before without even realizing it.

How to Hug a Monster is the first warm-up exercise. All
seven warm-up exercises are connected, and each one
builds upon the next. They are intended to help set a

process in motion. Deceptively simple at first glance, they are about establishing and/or clarifying your relationship to some difficult and exciting concepts: pleasure and pain, dreams and fears, success and failure, prosperity and lack—all the stuff that monsters feed on.

When you hug a monster, you forever alter the pattern of your life and experience a fresh blast of energy at the center of your being. That's the immediate payoff. Additional payoffs may be in store as well, but they tend to show up in the general quality of your life, rather than in a flash of instant transformation.

I don't believe there is such a thing as instant transformation, although it is a very popular myth. We are a culture that, for decades, has been in hot pursuit of some final destination that we hope marks our ultimate arrival as successful people. It's as if we actually believe a day will come when we can say, "There. Now I've got it," believing we have touched ultimate truth and will never again be in the dark, alone and afraid. The fact is, very few of us experience inner growth and change as a lightning bolt. Nature doesn't work that way. The lightning bolt carries such intensity, we often don't account for the months or years of work that generated it. Real change is a process going on in the context of your total life, and not an isolated moment. Yet there are skills, strategies, and tools to support you and make your growth enjoyable and, perhaps, a little more rapid.

Monsters come in a variety of species, and this section is also about helping you learn to recognize them no matter where they happen to be hanging out. They can exist anywhere and under any circumstances, and they thrive on conflict of all kinds. Whatever is important to you, you can safely assume a monster or two is lurking nearby. The more you know about yourself, the more you'll know about your monsters.

The Monster Families

What are the most common kinds of inner conflicts, or monsters? In order to answer that question, we first have to take a look at the *contexts* within which we live our lives. Essentially, there are three: the self, others, and our environment. Our relative ease and dis-ease come from the way we understand and interact within them.

Using these contexts—self, others, and environment—we looked for and named major behaviors that show up again and again as monsters that most often block us from taking action, growing, and enjoying life to the fullest. Here is a quick summary of our monster families and their primary behaviors. They are discussed in greater depth in the sections named for them.

• *Inertia Monsters* are anywhere in our lives that we have allowed routines to become ruts and habits.

• *Logic Monsters* hang out in the "real world" where we act only on what we can see, touch, and name. They cause us to lose the ability to act on an impulse, be creative, use our intuition, or be playful. Logic monsters keep us in our heads and out of our hearts.

• *Relationship Monsters* show up in a multitude of circumstances that involve conflicts with other people.

• *Freedom Monsters* find all kinds of reasons for holding back in life, and their favorite words are security, control, responsibility, and predictability.

• *Eternal Monsters* stand between us and our spiritual lives. According to many experienced inner explorers, from psychologists to mystics, these are the most powerful monsters of all. To hug them requires facing an ultimate mystery of our being . . . our mortality.

Putting Together Your Own *Hug the Monster* Program

To be physically fit, you exercise your entire body, not just your arms or your legs, right? A *Hug the Monster* exercise program works the same way. To make sure you are working with your fears, attitudes, and behaviors in a balanced way, we recommend creating sets of exercises, selecting at least one from each of the five monster families. This is to avoid the temptation of doing only those that seem the easiest, and to make sure you get the maximum "cross-training" benefit that comes from being willing to face *any* fear, not just a few kinds of fears.

In the back of the book you'll find an index of all of the exercises and their corresponding monsters. Once you've begun your *Hug the Monster* exercise program, you can use it as a way to review your progress at a glance, noting those you've completed and those you have yet to begin. As a record of your total experience with *Hug the Monster*, it can also help you do your exercises in sets and keep you on track with your commitments.

Ideally, you'll use a notebook or journal to help you track your progress, record your commitments, and express the insights you discover as you explore all of the exercises.

Important: Do the warm-up exercises for yourself and not for someone else's approval. We all mature at different rates, stimulated by a variety of life experiences. Sometimes a major event such as moving, getting a divorce, losing a job, or the death of a loved one is the trigger to begin a process of discarding the values of our childhood environment. Sometimes, circumstances beyond our control force us to deal with our fears. Other times, we make decisions that will bring us face to face with the monsters that we need to confront. Most often, it is the slow distillation over time—the ups and downs of life—that leads us to discover what is uniquely our own view of the world.

Turning on the Lights, Looking Under the Bed

Remember the monsters that lived in your bedroom as a kid? They were in the closet, under the bed, on the ceiling, or tapping on the windowsill. They were powerful in the dark and impotent during the day. To make them disappear was easy at night. The flick of a light switch or a comforting word from Mom or Dad would do it every time. Did you talk yourself out of them, scare yourself to death by watching them haunt your room—or did you just turn on the lights? The series of questions that follows is like that light switch. It will take you in the direction of daytime reality, en route to your waking dreams.

And while we're on the subject of childhood, when you were a kid did you spend endless hours daydreaming about what your life would be like as a grown-up? Now and then it is good to check in with that ten-year-old version of yourself. In what ways does the life that you imagined compare with the one you've lived so far? If there's something back there you haven't outgrown, discarded, or given up on yet, now is the time to bring it forward.

Once you've completed all seven of the following warm-up exercises, go back and reflect on your responses. You've just created a self-portrait, and a good frame of reference for the "old" you. Make sure you've dated the pages if you are keeping a journal. Some day you'll enjoy rereading them, realizing just how much you've grown and how far you've come.

Warm-Up Exercise 1. How to Hug a Monster
Monster: Planning for Success

What kind of a risk taker are you? *Recall a successful event in your past that involved taking action even though you were afraid.* What was your process? How did it change your life? Find the biggest one you can think of. Candidates would include changing careers, quitting your job, getting married or divorced, buying a house, starting a business, moving to a new city, going back to college, or anything that meant you had to calculate the risk and take action where the outcome wasn't known—where your security, identity, or comfort was momentarily threatened.

Compare your process to the five steps involved in How to Hug a Monster. What kind of monster was it? If it involved procrastination or being stuck in a rut, that's an *Inertia Monster*. Perhaps it had to do with your relationship to another person—a *Relationship Monster*. Did the risk mean defying "facts" with a creative or intuitive impulse? If so, it was a *Logic Monster* you hugged. You hugged a *Freedom Monster* if you realized your so-called security was actually a ball and chain, and you took a daring leap in the direction of fun and adventure. If you hugged an *Eternal Monster*, there's no doubt your life changed in deep and meaningful ways.

How to Hug a Monster

1. Gather Information
    Keys: Assessment, Strategy, Flexibility
2. Develop the Skill
    Keys: Two Laps, Self-Discipline, Failure
        as Feedback
3. Set the Date
4. Don't Think about It, Just Hug It
5. Reflect

Which of the five steps listed here did you follow? Which ones weren't part of your process? Which ones were difficult? Easy? Is there a pattern in the way you tend to act when you are afraid and the stakes are high? In other words, in your successful risk, did you procrastinate for years before acting, refusing to set a date? Did you avoid doing research, throwing caution to the wind, acting on sheer impulse? Would you have been more successful if only you had invested the time in gaining more skill? Have you thought about it much since then, or do you think reflection is not a productive use of your time? If it is useful to you, record your thoughts in your journal.

Exercise
Part One:
Recall a time you hugged a monster, comparing your process with our five step method.

Part Two:
List your biggest successes.

Warm-Up Exercise 2. Beautiful Dreamer
Monster: Lack of Direction

> *Dreams: Meaningful, motivating aims that seem*
> *attainable, but are beyond your immediate grasp.*

What are your unfulfilled dreams? Just about everyone I've ever met has a basket full of things they long to experience. Consider everything from lifelong dreams to yesterday's inspiration. What about the talents that you have never fully developed, far off lands you've fantasized about visiting, and professional achievements you yearn to accomplish? Think about your childhood, your partner, your kids, and your friends. Immerse yourself as if it were all possible . . . physically, financially, emotionally, professionally. Don't hold back. Imagine it all.

What might be stopping you from having those experiences we call dreams? Is it a very nameable fear? Or is it merely a lack of energy, enthusiasm, resources, and/or imagination? Whatever you do, don't hold yourself back, and while you are at it, don't edit yourself. Reflect upon your dreams and begin looking forward to living each and every one of them, imagining how you might feel when you live them.

Exercise

Part One:
Write down everything you've ever wanted to do. Fill the page with dreams.

Part Two:
From all of those dreams, choose the ten you love the most.

Part Three:
Finally, select and highlight three dreams from your list of ten that you intend to focus on for your *Hug the Monster* program.

Warm-Up Exercise 3. Yikes!
Monster: Fears

Fears: Strong feelings caused by expecting harm.

What are your biggest fears? Consider everything from heights, embarrassment, and speaking in public to losing your job, illness, loneliness, and failure. Do you worry about old age? Financial security? Being alone? Not being a hero in your kid's eyes? Never having free time to relax or take a vacation? Being more successful than your partner or other family members? Do you tremble at the thought of riding in an elevator, getting on an airplane, or confronting spiders in the bathtub? Do you avoid parties because you are shy? Whatever you are afraid of is fair game for this inventory.

Look for a connection between your dreams and your fears. Have your dreams stalled because of these fears? How can your fears energize your dreams? What might it mean to Hug the Monster if every fear on your list is blocking your path and threatening your long-term happiness and success?

Is fear real? Yes, and no. Let's say you are rappelling down the side of a mountain. If the rope breaks, you fall through the air seven hundred feet. That's a scary thought, so subjectively, the fear is real. But the rope is strong enough to hold the weight of a truck. The chances of it breaking are very remote. Objectively, the fear is a lie. It is based upon ignorance. Here's another example. Let's say you are painfully shy, and you have to staff your company's trade-show booth. The thought of talking to strangers triggers anxiety. But in reality, the people at the trade show won't hurt you. In all likelihood, they'll be full of questions about your products and services, and conversation will come easily. The odds of shyness being a huge problem are very slim. In these contexts, here's my favorite definition of F.E.A.R.: False Evidence Appearing Real.

It is quite possible that you aren't fully aware of your fears, so this may be an essential discovery for you to make. Take the time to make a list of your fears. Go for the whoppers. As you do this exercise, notice where the fear is objective, and where it is subjective—where gaining more information will end ignorance, abate the fear, and move you toward your dreams.

Exercise

Part One:
Write down everything you feel fear over. Fill a blank page with your fears, dreads, and anxieties.

Part Two:
From all of those fears, choose ten you really want to embrace, and list them.

Part Three:
Finally, select and highlight three fears from your list of ten that you intend to focus on for your *Hug the Monster* program.

Warm-Up Exercise 4. I Gotta Be Me
Monster: Inner Conflict

*Personal Values: Core concepts of high personal
worth that give our lives meaning.*

Time is a nonrenewable resource. Becoming totally clear
about the value of a single day can be transformative all by
itself. As the Mad Hatter scolded the folks of Wonderland,
"If you knew time as well as I do, you wouldn't talk about
wasting it." The way you spend your time is a reflection of
your values, and a measure of how well you know yourself. More than two thousand years ago, Sophocles wrote,
"One must wait until the evening to see how splendid the
day has been." To the best of our ability, we prioritize our
days based upon those things which are most important to
us—our true values.

But we have demands on our time. Somewhere along
the line, life starts living us, instead of the other way
around. For example: We may say we value freedom above
all else, but find ourselves in a profession where we are en-
slaved by the work. We may say we value family, but
spend our time in ways which produce financial security
and never yield a single family vacation, let alone deep and
lasting emotional satisfaction. An authentic life emerges
from questioning the values of our parents, mentors, and
peers, and constructing values that each of us alone can
embrace with our entire being. Values tend to change with
maturity and life experience.

I discovered long ago that *when my actions are aligned
with my values, my life is beautiful* because there can be no
conflict inside of me. Sure there are obstacles, but overcoming them is part of what I value. What about you? Do

your actions align with your values? Take note of how you spend your time and then list your values. Do you find conflict or harmony here? Is your life in balance?

Exercise

Part One: What are your values?

Think about what is really important to you and note as many things as possible. Candidates might be telling the truth, saving money for your children's future, exercising to stay fit and healthy, spending time alone, spending time with friends, going to your place of worship, being politically active, etc. They might also include things such as laughing, playing golf, eating delicious food, enjoying great films, books, or music, being adventurous in all things, or riding your bicycle. Be as specific as possible so you can notice the enjoyment and value at the heart of every activity.

Part Two: Draw a circle

Place the ten most important values inside a circle, representing your own center, the place from which you intend to live your life.

Part Three: Commit to three

Highlight those values you do not yet fully live, but would like to.

Warm-Up Exercise 5. Both Sides Now
Monster: Lack of Clarity

What really bugs you?

What bugs you about life? What makes you feel anxious? What takes a good mood and turns it sour, makes you lose your patience, and steals your time, energy, and imagination? Go with the first things that come to your mind. You might write down "slow drivers in the fast lane, rainy weather, politicians, and high prices at the grocery store." Don't over analyze. There'll be plenty of time for that later. Just write them down.

What do you love about your life?

For every irritation in life there are plenty of joys. What and who makes you smile? When do you find yourself feeling satisfied and peaceful inside? What energizes you the most? Consider your daily life, capture some happy images, and translate them into a list of what you love about your life. "When my son and I ride mountain bikes together, swimming in the ocean after the initial cold shock, seeing my daughter perform in a play, watching the 49ers play on Sunday afternoons," would be examples.

Exercise

List ten things that bug you most in life, and ten things that you love most about your life.

Warm-Up Exercise 6. Personal Balance Sheet
Monster: Denial

Ben Franklin kept a personal diary of behaviors and habits he wanted to change, and he reportedly worked to change them, one at a time, until he'd successfully defeated each shortcoming.

Life demands that we repeat certain behaviors daily, and some would argue that we can't always be conscious of every act. When we repeat actions unconsciously, or without much thought, they are called habits. These unconscious habits we have developed over time are the most difficult ones to recognize and bring to the surface to work on. We often have elaborate defense mechanisms to keep them buried—in other words, we spend a lot of unconscious energy denying their existence.

In order to work on them, we need to examine our habits. The good habits produce wanted results, and bad habits cost us the progress we would otherwise enjoy. If you always get up at six A.M. and get to work on time, that could be considered a good habit. Flossing, eating right, and exercising would also fall into this category. Perhaps you drink a little too much, or watch too much TV, or indulge in sports to the point of compulsion. Things that steal your time, numb your creativity, and damage your health are easy candidates for the bad-habits list. Go for it. Face them here by listing ten *each*. It is important to own our strengths as well as our weaknesses. In order to face this monster, rigorous honesty is in order. As you develop this self-assessment skill, more will come to the surface.

Exercise

List ten strengths and ten weaknesses. Then highlight the three most important ones in each category—those that will most likely be involved in hugging monsters most often.

Warm-Up Exercise 7. The Wheel of Fortune
Monster: Money

This exercise isn't about how to have more money, it's about having a great life and the role money may or may not play. I've never amassed a fortune. Yet I can't help but feel I must be doing something right. I can honestly say that money, or the lack of it, has never stopped me from doing the things I want to do.

Almost everyone has money monsters, so let's cut to the chase. *What would make your life wonderful?* Where does your mind go first when you imagine it? To material possessions you desire such as houses, cars, and clothes? To experiences you long to have, such as travel or professional achievements? To people you'd prefer to be with? To an inner state of being? More time to do the things you love? Can you mentally construct the elements that you believe would make your life wonderful?

Our *relationship* to money is the point. Is it a lifestyle you are after, or a life? I look at money as a form of energy, as a resource. The word *affluent* in its root form means "flow." Hugging monsters—successfully dealing with inner conflict—increases our enjoyment in life. *Flow happens*. It isn't necessary to have lots of money in order to be affluent. Time, energy, and imagination are powerful resources, often buying what money can't. In my experience, the resources we need flow from innovation, and not the other way around. Perhaps even "downsizing" is a blessing in disguise, showing us the joy in a simpler life.

The money monster reminds me of that cutting, often-quoted George Bernard Shaw line, "There are two tragedies in life. One is to lose your heart's desire. The other is to gain it." When the Buddha first became enlightened, he realized that it is human nature to desire and suffer over not only that which we don't have, but also that which we have, because once we have it, we fear losing it.

What do you love to do? Without any money, would you stop doing it? No way! You'd figure out a way to trade, barter, shop a little bit harder, or save a little bit longer in order to get around your financial obstacle. If you won the lottery, would you stop doing the things you love to do? Not a chance.

One last thought on the subject. The future is an idea. Experiences are in the present moment. "Wonderful" is an experience. If you are honest with yourself, you realize that "wonderful" is only in the present. There's a lot of myth and ignorance in the world when it comes to money, so don't necessarily take advice from anyone. *Forget everything you were ever taught about money in your childhood. What have you experienced as true in your own life?*

Exercise

Part One:

Make a list of everything you fret over where money is concerned, and examine it for lurking monsters. Money may be a camouflage issue for Inertia Monsters, Logic Monsters, Freedom Monsters, Relationship Monsters, or even the Eternal Monsters.

Part Two:

Write down all of the things that would make your life wonderful in two categories—the present, and the future. Notice the differences or similarities between the two lists.

Part Three:

Highlight those items on your lists that you could take corrective or assertive action on right away if you were motivated to do so.

Chapter Three

The Inertia Monsters

Exercise	Monster
1. Go to Work a New Way	**Breaking Routine**
2. Climb Any Mountain	**Being Stuck in Place**
3. A Week without TV	**Wasting Time**
4. Alter Your Environment	**Stagnation**
5. Do It Now	**Procrastination**
6. Fail/Get Rejected	**Instant Gratification**
7. Break an Addiction	**False Security**
8. Life Is Delicious	**Lack of Curiosity**
9. A Rose by Any Other Name	**Labels and Limits**
10. Surprise Yourself	**Being Rigid**
11. Ask for Help	**False Pride**

Inertia Monsters are like dandelions in spring—they are both common and prolific. The dandelions' bright yellow flowers broadcast their presence beautifully, but if we don't remove them quickly, they turn to seed and multiply. Corrective action is always temporary. Constant vigilance is the key. I'm not aware of any lawn service for Inertia Monsters. But like all things in nature, they serve a purpose. Dandelion roots are believed by some to have medicinal properties. Inertia Monsters are good for us, too. They show up to suggest we need to take action. But if they move in, get fat and comfortable, they sap our energy and take over. Bigger problems are sure to follow.

Webster's defines *inert* as "not having the power to move itself." Inertia Monsters have the power *if you hug them*. Preparing taxes. Cleaning the garage. Exercising.

Completing a big project at work. You have your list and I
have mine. We know the dread, and we know the satisfaction of finally getting things done.

Perhaps Inertia Monsters are a form of childlike rebel-
lion, or an expression of the perfectionist in you, or the
daredevil in you that loves the adrenaline rush of barely
making a deadline. The ability to prioritize, discipline
yourself, and enjoy whatever task is yours to accomplish
comes with practice. In the end, Do It Now is the only way.
But we can trick ourselves into being grown-ups about
tackling our responsibilities and fulfilling our commitments if we're willing to get a little creative and, like
pulling up the roots, search for what's underneath the inertia. The following exercises will help you do just that.

While all fifty-two exercises in *Hug the Monster* are intended to help us become more flexible and energetic, these
exercises are specifically designed as remedies for boredom, routine, and life in a rut.

Exercise 1. Go to Work a New Way
Monster: Breaking Routine

As a student at the University of West Florida in Pen-
sacola, I once kayaked to school, a memorable little misadventure among several I've experienced in my career. It
meant navigating out of a bayou, through a sound, onto a
river, and into a tributary on campus. The distance was further than I thought (not enough advance preparation), and
due to a fasting regimen I was on at the time, I developed
wrenching abdominal muscle cramps. Only when spasms
were jerking my body and I was near capsizing did I realize the water was full of alligators! "How embarrassing to

die a half mile from campus," I thought. With great effort, I relaxed my mind and body and made it safely to my destination.

I also lived in New York for twelve years. I used to enjoy running, walking, or biking to meetings instead of taking a taxi or accepting a ride in someone's car. After having four bicycles stolen, I eventually walked into meetings with my briefcase in one hand and my bike slung over my shoulder.

If our lives are like music, then our routines and rituals are the melody line, providing theme and structure, bringing order out of chaos. Coffee with the morning paper is a ritual that signals the start of a new day for lots of people. Can you make a distinction between your routines and your habits? *Awareness* is the key. When does a useful routine become a mindless habit? I've never had a traditional nine-to-five office job, yet I've still managed to find myself in routines that, if I'm not careful, are mindless instead of stimulating and creative. The willingness to take risks has to do with how often you break your routines in other ways, and how much and how deep the habits in your life affect the quality of your daily living. You'll be far more likely to take healthy risks once you enjoy breaking the little patterns that have the illusion of defining your life.

How to Go to Work a New Way

However you normally go to work, alter your routine . . . your route, your method of transportation, your conversation if you ride/carpool with others, your thoughts if you go alone. Do it for a day, then for a full week. Can you keep it up for an entire month?

If you go to the same place every day, there are plenty

of things you can do to break routine and wake yourself up. There's not much fear accompanying this one, but if you don't watch it, you can put yourself to sleep by doing things the same way all of the time. How many different ways are there to go to work? Here are a few more examples. With radio on. And off. With tapes. Public transportation. Carpool. Back roads. Dressed up. Not dressed up. Driving straight there, not driving straight there. Normally take coffee? Try tea, orange juice, or mineral water. Leave at different times of the day. What about jogging, biking, or blading to work once in a while? (Note: If there is no place to shower at work, don't let that stop you. Why not talk to management and see what can be done to support physical fitness at work? Even talking to management may constitute a break in your routine!)

Think about the other routines in your life where mindless driving comes into play. How many routes are there for getting to the grocery store? To a friend's home? To the fitness club? Have you ever walked, biked, or skated there instead of driving? Get creative and you'll instantly feel alive.

> *And the trouble is, if you don't risk anything,*
> *you risk even more.*   —Erica Jong

Exercise 2. Climb Any Mountain
Monster: Being Stuck in Place

The first mountain I ever climbed was the famous Matterhorn in the Swiss Alps. Although climbing it involves some degree of technical difficulty, many people don't realize that it is a relatively easy thing to do for experienced mountain climbers. For a beginner like me, it was an ambitious adventure. Before we began, my guides winced when I proudly showed off my new climbing boots. They warned me about the hazards of not breaking them in first, but I didn't listen. I was too eager to climb the irresistible peak that, from down below, draws your gaze to it like a powerful magnet. To be there and not climb it was unthinkable. During the climb I developed bleeding blisters on my feet. I fell several times, too, and even though I was tied to a rope, the sensation of falling was pretty scary. In spite of the pain and with plenty of encouragement from my guides, I was rewarded for my endurance when, just below the summit, I leaned against the face of the mountain and looked out at the vast expanse of alpine majesty. Surprisingly perhaps, the richness of the visual scene combined with the intensity of the physical challenge also makes you *listen* intently. There is a certain prayerful quality to the absolute stillness from the top of a mountain that is unlike the silence anywhere else I've ever been. It is pure and full. It wasn't until I reached that spot that I felt I understood the passion that drives mountain climbers to risk so much for the experience.

We're often reminded that success is in the journey and not in the destination. I don't agree. It's both. To separate them is a mistake. If you stand at the bottom and wonder, "What's it like up there?" it's a start, but you must move immediately. Most of my adventures have begun with a desire to have a new experience. There are many ways to climb. Perhaps you've always wanted the thrill of riding the biggest, scariest roller coaster in town, and to do it you need only climb the steps to get in the line at the amusement park.

As a metaphor for breaking out of a comfort zone,

"climb" can represent just about anything that's both new to you and a little bit frightening. But taken literally, climbing clears cobwebs, stretches muscles, and strengthens resolve faster than many other activities.

Climbing as a metaphor means moving toward something that might not be attainable . . . toward the unknown, toward something you might not even see. Rock climbers can't always see beyond their next move. Mountain climbers and experienced hikers are fooled by false summits constantly, yet they know to keep moving. False summits, if taken as true summits, threaten our success and/or safety. Psychologically, when we think the end is near, we sometimes relax prematurely. Or we give everything, only to realize we must give a little more. It happens in business, in sport, and at home. In life the top is rarely *the* top. A risk taker is always motivated to take on the next challenge.

Especially when we feel depressed, isolated, or afraid, motivation to climb is hard to find. Pulling ourselves out of a deep pit like indebtedness, failure, disappointment, or crippling low self-esteem is probably an inevitable part of a full, rewarding life. The important thing isn't that you are down, it's that you know you can climb. How will you know it? By doing these exercises, you can get out of your head and move, and look forward to a second wind.

How to do Climb Any Mountain

Option One: Climb a mountain.

If you live near mountains, the exercise is obvious. Do your homework and plan a day of hiking and climbing. We don't mean the technical kind where equipment and advanced skill is required. This is nontechnical. Yet, if you've never gone hiking and climbing before, invite an experienced hiker to come along with you. Set a date, then prepare for it. Learn what clothing and equipment you'll need, what provisions you can carry comfortably in a day pack such as water, energy bars, sunscreen, a pocketknife, and an extra layer of clothing for changing weather. Study maps of the trails that will take you upward.

Option Two: Climb the highest building.

For city dwellers, this is even simpler. Identify the tallest building in town and promise yourself you'll climb the stairs. Make it an adventure. Pack a lunch. Plan to meet friends. Time yourself and repeat the climb several times, each time doing it faster and better.

Option Three: Climb a tree.

Live in the suburbs? Go to a city, state, or national park. Scout out the trees and find the one you want to climb. Practice pull-ups on a nearby limb. Take this exercise seriously by planning, preparing, and setting the date. Invite friends or go alone, but set your sights on the top and get there!

Whatever you decide to climb, remember to use your mind and heart along with your body. Use your climb as a time to imagine you are moving closer to your dreams and goals with every step and hand movement. Along the way, stop and assess how far you've come. Congratulate yourself on your progress. Pay attention to the amount of fear or anxiety you started with, and any that may still be lingering. When you get to the top, enjoy the view. Then, when you get back on the ground, ask yourself which part was better: anticipating it, doing it, or being at the top. My guess is that you'll answer: *all of the above.*

Each fresh peak ascended teaches something.
—Sir Martin Conway

Exercise 3. A Week Without TV
Monster: Wasting Time

My father was a doctor and someone I thoroughly admired and respected. During a period in my life when I
was particularly anti-television, I walked into my father's
living room while he was watching a very stupid show,
with his dinner on a TV tray in front of him. "Why are you
watching that?" I asked incredulously. He replied, "Well, I
have to eat, don't I?" Here was this extremely intelligent
guy, locked into some low-grade, mind-numbing habit. I
never forgot it.

The *Detroit Free Press*, as part of a research project, once
paid people to turn off their TVs, and in short order, the
honest ones were returning their paychecks, unable to sustain the practice beyond a few days. What if television
weren't there to hypnotize, entertain, and pacify you? What
conversations would you have? What books or magazines
would you read? What great meditative thoughts might
bubble up? How would your food taste?! Socially accept-
able habits sanctioned by almost everyone are often the
most insidious. Now and then it is healthy to question
everything you do. A week without television might just
add brand new layers of stimulation, interest, and skill to
your life. When you return to the TV, you'll be wiser in TV
time management.

How to do A Week Without TV

Part One: Plan ahead.

If you are a hard-core television junkie, you may have
to prepare for this exercise. For one week, calculate the
number of hours you spend in front of the tube. This in it-

self is a turnoff. Scope out the week by making plans in advance for people you'll visit, errands, shopping, or repairs that need to be done.

Part Two: Turn it off and pull the plug.

And while you are at it, include the radio as well. Read the newspaper. Invent a project to accomplish. What have you been procrastinating over lately? Get busy with three other *Hug the Monster* exercises to fill your time. There's no time like the present, especially with the television unplugged. Things to consider: How many hours of your life get invested in front of the tube, and what do you get in exchange? How much and what kind of food would you *not* consume if you didn't watch TV? What relationships could be enhanced? What great stories or games could you invent with your kids? What would the furniture arrangement in your living room look like without a big screen or a little box?

> *Cherish forever what makes you unique, 'cuz you're really a yawn if it goes!* —Bette Midler

Exercise 4. Alter Your Environment
Monster: Stagnation

As a professional adventurer, I am constantly stimulated and totally captivated by my surroundings, and have found it easy to feel at home just about anywhere because of it. It comes naturally to me, and I realize I'm very lucky. Whether it is the rugged landscapes of Peru, mud dung huts in Kenya, or the stars over the Sahara Desert, I draw my inspiration from what I hear, see, and feel around me.

Altering my environment charges my system like nothing else can, allowing me to live the life of an adventurer with success and comfort, viewing the entire planet as my playground, my home, and my office. On the other hand, I am more prone to clutter and mess around the house and must continually monitor the ratio of order to chaos around me. Being neat and orderly isn't my natural talent, but I recognize the benefits in increased productivity. Environment definitely contributes to how life moves or gets blocked. Some say environment actually mirrors the flow of energy for the creatures who inhabit a place, and that we can know a lot about ourselves by studying our environments.

Home is a fundamental reality for most creatures on Earth, but before it is an address, home is an ideal that invites bringing all of what one values into a place to which one may return again and again for emotional and spiritual balance, and physical and psychological nourishment. In nature, species survive or perish based upon their ability to adapt to the changing environment. In business and commerce the same is true—adaptability is essential in order to compete, grow, and prosper. Depending upon how strongly you identify your "self" with your environment, the results of this exercise range from fun to profound. *Where is your center, and who are you, really?* Nature seems to be teaching us that outer and inner surroundings change, and so must we in order to grow.

How to do Alter Your Environment

For this exercise, you are going to make some changes in your immediate environment. Target your work space first, since this is probably the place in which fresh, creative thoughts need to be seeded and nurtured. Work should involve playfulness. Where are your toys? In the ancient Chinese art *feng shui,* one considers the placement of all furnishings and objects as a statement about the flow of energy in the home or workplace. Can you transform the influence of your work environment to enhance not only the cosmetic appearance, but the way you feel while you are there? It further suggests that comfort and success in everyday living have a great deal to do with the way our environments affect us. What is your current work space saying about you? Do you see the inner you expressed in the "outer you"?

Add greenery, color, and fresh scents to your space with flowering plants. If you aren't sure how to do that, go to a florist or nursery and get advice. Are your dreams too far out of reach? Get maps and posters from travel companies and hang them where you'll be inspired nonstop. Are you too organized? Get messy. Are you always messy? Get organized. Stir things up a bit. Change the color on the floors, walls, and ceilings. Add natural potpourri to make things smell nice. There are scores of ways to alter your environment to get those creative juices flowing. Tour open houses on Sunday afternoons, scan magazines and books, or visit hotels in search of better, more productive, warm, friendly, supportive spaces.

> I sometimes wonder what sort of quality my work
> would have if I worked in a harsh, rectangular,
> smooth-surfaced, evenly lit glossy office.
> —Christopher Day, architect,
> author of *Places of the Soul*

Exercise 5. Do It Now
Monster: Procrastination

Lost Horizon, by James Hilton, is the romantic story of an idyllic place called Shangri-La where people enjoy extraordinary health and longevity. Although Hilton's book is fiction, there is a real-life spot high in the Himalayas called Hunza, where lack of exposure to the diseases, wars, and crimes of modern civilization contributes to the inhabitants' ability to live healthy, productive lives well beyond one hundred years of age. As soon as I learned about Hunza, I wanted to go. But it took me ten years to finally get there.

Hunza, I learned, wasn't a place you just booked a flight to. A political hot spot, it is situated twelve miles from the former USSR while sharing borders with China, Kashmir, Pakistan, and Afghanistan. People told me I'd never gain entry, and I was just about to concede the point when my determination generated good fortune. *Geo* magazine granted me an assignment, adding urgency and motivation to the challenge of getting there. After years of working through proper and improper channels to gain a visa, I decided to abandon those efforts and take matters into my own hands. I flew to Islamabad, the capital of Pakistan. In the government Office of Information, I met and chatted with a portly ex–cricket player who was both interested in physical fitness and sympathetic to my request. We made a trade: I gave him a regimen of physical fitness exercises, and he gave me a visa to enter Hunza.

Most people would agree that a "do it now" philosophy is great. Yet as with so many of the *Hug the Monster* exercises, taking an intellectual position or following the advice of other people isn't enough. Notice the words. They don't say "think about it now." Or "do it later." You've got to find your motivation, and have some sense of the payoff involved. If you don't take what you're doing seriously, it is easy to justify delaying. It is true that self-discipline requires practice. The interesting thing is, if it is important enough to you to serve up a good dose of procrastination, then there is probably something very important in the activity for you to discover. This is the way to disarm the Inertia Monster. He's holding something in his hand, and it is your job to find out what that is.

You'll need to get underneath the inertia, to discover why you aren't moving forward. Here are some of the most common causes. Are you procrastinating because you tend to be a *perfectionist,* and you rationalize not beginning until the perfect time and circumstance? Forget that one, because perfect isn't real. Do you love the adrenaline rush of a near miss and prefer burning midnight oil as time runs out so you can be *heroic* in your accomplishment? Is it a *rebellious nature* that feeds the delays, defying whatever authority is involved? Is the task just so awfully painful or disagreeable that the thought of it puts you off? And finally, are you merely *indecisive,* waiting for more of whatever you think you need, thereby justifying your nonaction? Because motivation is the ultimate key, How to Hug a Monster works really well, so follow the five steps we offered you in Warm-Up Exercise 1. Finally, build in a fabulous reward for yourself. Here's a little tip that writers use when we know getting started is three-quarters of the victory. It's called the Write Garbage Rule. It means lower your standards, *temporarily.*

How to do Do It Now

Step One: Do the hard part first.

Write down the things you always put off. Next to each task that you are presently procrastinating over, list the benefit from getting it done and the reward you'll give yourself. Get creative on the payoff. What would you really love to treat yourself to when the job is done? Declare the date, and don't set yourself up for failure by making it too far in the future, or so immediate that odds of success are astronomical. Refer to the five-step method. Do you need more information? Get it. Skill? Start practicing.

Step Two: Get a buddy to help.

Share your list with someone, and ask them to support you by regularly asking about your progress. Make a timeline if necessary, but agree to talk regularly. Reward them by including them in the payoff.

> *I missed all of the shots I never took.*
> —Wayne Gretsky, professional hockey player

Exercise 6. Fail/Get Rejected
Monster: Instant Gratification

In my business, the difference between an amateur and professional is a paycheck. Early in my career, I realized I would have to blaze new trails in business in addition to the ones I pioneered as an adventurer. Convincing people to sponsor me meant being able to communicate my vision to Madison Avenue ad agencies and their corporate clients. It meant learning how to make cold calls and warm contacts, how to navigate the protective maze of secretaries and administrative assistants who, like sentries, guarded the entrance to the playing fields where decisions were made. I moved from San Francisco to New York City for greater access, and quickly learned the benefits of hearing rejections: "No" is what happens on the way to "yes." I started enjoying the process as an opportunity to hear constructive feedback and to meet people. Whenever I had an adventure that needed a sponsor, I would put together a list of prospects and call on the *least likely* one first. In other words, I would plan on being rejected, and then go to school on what I learned in the process of hearing "No, thanks." Each meeting improved my presentation for the next. As my list of contacts increased, so did my success in finding sponsors for my adventures.

We think we will die of embarrassment if we are rejected. We sometimes don't even get up to bat because we don't want to strike out. The way I understand it, success and failure, as commonly spoken of, are really impostors. *It is the experience of moving toward the goal that is important.* Moving equals success. Not moving equals failure.

The best salespeople know that success in making cold calls is an odds game. Many of them use a ratio of calls to sales. If it takes ten calls to make a sale, they are eager to get on the phone because it means they are getting closer to the payoff with every rejection. Author and business guru, Tom Peters, preaches the need for business schools to offer courses in failure, because he knows the tremendous value in learning to accept feedback for what it is. IBM's chairman Tom Watson Jr. once commented, "If you want to succeed, double your failure rate."

Let's call it *expectation management*. When you expect instant gratification, you put a lot of pressure on yourself. When we dream big dreams, the pressure mounts even more, and the stakes seem high. Impatient for a short-term payoff, we try to trick the odds. Instant gratification is almost always a monster keeping us from deeper, long-lasting success built upon the rock-solid foundation of persistence, practice, and skill development. Expect to succeed through a process. Don't expect a home run in your first at bat.

How to do Fail / Get Rejected

You are about to discover the benefits of being rejected. First, you must choose the activity. Here are some thoughts to get you going. What idea have you been keeping to yourself for fear of ridicule or rejection? Have you written something you think is pretty good, but no one has ever read? Have you developed a strategy or possible solution to a problem at home or work no one has ever heard about? Have you thought about starting a business on the side, but the fear of selling is holding you back? Do you only sing in the shower even though you'd like to do it for an audience? Is there someone you'd like to ask on a date, but the thought of hearing "no" triggers a retreat to the sofa with a TV dinner? Now is the time to take action, and to learn you won't die from a little bit of rejection.

Just remember this: "No" is what happens on the way to "yes." So put it out there! Mail your poems or short stories to magazines, and get as many rejection slips as you can. Share your ideas with five people at work. Sing your heart out at a karaoke bar. Demonstrate your invention to a committee of your friends. Use the five-step method and get as many rejections as possible in a single week.

> *It takes a lot of courage to show your dreams*
> *to someone else.*   —Erma Bombeck

Exercise 7. Break an Addiction
Monster: False Security

Years ago, I owned a bar, and I loved to party. I drank and smoked cigarettes. These days, my act is pretty clean from a health standpoint (although I love black tea with milk and sugar). I'm not going to lecture on the merits or drawbacks of any particular vice or addiction. Carl Jung said, "Every form of addiction is bad, no matter whether the narcotic be alcohol, or morphine, or idealism." To me, that's an interesting statement about human nature. To the degree we are addicted to anything, we are not free. Our choices are limited if we think we cannot live or be happy *without* a certain anything. To be free we must also be free of addictions—things that have power to compel us to act . . . seemingly against our will. My goals as a swimmer made it relatively easy to let go of the cigarette habit. It was pretty simple logic. In order to swim great distances, I could no longer smoke. The more I swam, the less I had the urge to grab for a cigarette. I soon became a nonsmoker and a nondrinker.

For our purposes here, habits and addictions are similar issues. Experts on human behavior suggest the best way to break an unwanted habit is not to focus on breaking the habit, but on replacing the unwanted behavior with a new one. It has also been said that it takes about thirty days to integrate a new behavior into our lives. The corrective action takes time to settle in. Before it does, our comfort zone alarms are continually ringing the alert that all is not right. In this sense, our addictions give us a false sense of security because they offer familiarity. Hugging monsters is about overriding these alarms and getting outside our comfort zones.

In other words, prolonged awareness, patience, and the short-term ability to endure discomfort are involved. In a twelve-step program, this ability to endure comes down to one day at a time. It seems to work, because the proliferation of the twelve-step method of overcoming addictions has no doubt saved thousands of lives. The good news is that human nature is prone to healing when we allow it and don't interfere with the natural process.

How to do Break an Addiction

Part One: Write all your addictions down.

Expand the definition of *addiction* to anything you do compulsively. Don't rationalize or second-guess yourself. If you aren't sure, put it on the list and find out. What's the telltale sign? If the thought of *not* doing it causes you to feel anxious, insecure, or fearful. You may have years of interesting work ahead, but that's okay. Obvious candidates are drugs, foods, and/or beverages you consume habitually; routines you don't easily deviate from, such as watching TV while you have dinner; fingernail biting; never missing an episode of your soap operas; or compulsive behaviors like being meticulous about your spotless desk or your physical appearance.

Part Two: Get a second opinion.

Ask someone who knows you well about any behaviors they observe in you that seem like unhealthy habits, compulsions, or addictions. If you wish, ask several people for their feedback. Ask one trustworthy person to be your *Hug the Monster* coach. His or her job is to encourage you, help you set the date, ask the difficult questions, and praise you for your progress along the way.

Part Three: Choose to kick one bona fide addiction.

Apply the five-step method, How to Hug a Monster. Along with reading up on the subject, your research may include conversations with someone who successfully ended an addiction. You may want to go to a twelve-step meeting and find out if group support is something that works well for you. Your skill development will take the form of smaller victories and baby steps. For example, replace your morning coffee with herbal tea every other day. Need to lose fifteen pounds? You'll be successful if you focus on five pounds at a time, and not the full fifteen. If you are compulsive about your appearance, go grocery shopping without combing your hair or putting on make-up. (This is far easier than *going to work* without makeup, but that would be the ultimate goal using this example.) Relieve the immediate pressure by embracing the "one day at a time" philosophy, while visualizing the "new you" for every baby step you take successfully.

If you can kick one, you can kick more than one. Be patient. The process is the same for all of them. You can do it!

You must do the thing you think you cannot do
—Eleanor Roosevelt

Exercise 8. Life Is Delicious
Monster: Lack of Curiosity

I **love foreign foods.** Eating what the locals eat is one of
the secrets to great travel experiences. Hopefully, global-
ization will never destroy the uniqueness and variety of
diets found in cultures all around the world. I've enjoyed
snails with the French, goulash with Hungarians, crocodile
on the Nile, and six-course meals using my hands with the
Moroccans. On a recent New Year's Eve in Benares, India, I
drank *chai* (tea) served to me by an exotic-looking holy man
who lived in a beautiful, small cave above the banks of the
Ganges river. I watched him boil the water in an old pan
that sat gently above a delicate fire, as he prepared this traditional Indian drink of black tea, milk, sugar, cloves, cin-
namon, and other spices. I worried about accepting his hos-
pitality because drinking water in India can be dangerous.
Sitting across from him in the dimly lit cave, I could only
trust that the water was really *boiling*. It was New Year's
Eve and we were committed to a toast, so with some hesi-
tation, I slowly took my first sip from the cup he offered
me. My fears were unnecessary. It turned out to be the best,
most delicious *chai* I enjoyed the entire six weeks I was in
India.

After years of being exposed to new tastes, I love the
fact that my children are more open than many adults to
the thrills and fun of slightly unusual foods. Recently, my
teenage son Daren prepared a feast of New Orleans fare
that included alligator sausage, Cajun creole, and sautéed
turtle. We celebrated my daughter Chelsea's fourteenth
birthday at her favorite Moroccan place in San Francisco,
where we sat on the floor and ate with our hands. Every-

one in our party dressed up with Moroccan-style scarves, peasant shirts, and other exotic dress.

Being a lifelong learner is fun. Obviously, a sense of curiosity can be developed toward just about anything. But because eating is universal, we've focused on dining experiences as a great place to begin. Perhaps you'll have curiosity brainstorms of your own after doing these exercises.

How to do Life is Delicious

Option One: A theme dinner party.

Create a dinner party for two or twenty guests . . . or just for your family members. Select a country for the theme. One possibility is to make assignments for all of the guests to make sure everyone gets involved. Consider food, beverages, clothing, music, decor, language, and accessories like special eating tools. Choose a specific time period in history. With a little research, you can leave the present and visit the past, such as the banquet halls of King Henry VIII's castle.

The idea is to express as much as you can about the country, the food, and the native language. With so many specialty shops and so much ethnic cuisine available these days, the hardest part will be making your selections. Visit various restaurants, interview the chefs, or attend ethnic fairs just to get warmed up. Carry out the theme from the invitations to the napkins, from the first course to the last, from the conversation to the after-dinner games. Be sure to set the date, otherwise it will be a research project with mere good intentions for hors d'oeuvres.

Option Two: "On my seventy-fifth birthday, I will . . ."

We all have foods that make us salivate at the mere thought of them, and they are probably loaded with fat and sugar. Want some support for healthier eating? Invent new, healthier versions of your favorite recipes by planning a potluck dinner where everyone must bring a covered dish in the low-fat, low-cal model. Everyone also agrees to bring their recipe printed on a three-by-five card for all of the guests. Before you serve the hors d'oeuvres, begin the party with a two-mile walk/jog/bike ride in the neighborhood, and end it by telling stories of how you want to celebrate your seventy-fifth birthday.

> *Cooking is like love. It should be entered into with abandon or not at all.*   —Harriet Van Horne

Exercise 9. A Rose by Any Other Name
Monster: Labels and Limits

The first important legacy our parents give us is the name we are called. If you love your name, you are grateful to them. If you hate it, you have two choices: Live with it, or change it. Throughout school and into adulthood, our names contribute to our identities. For years I was known as Dave. But as my inner self evolved and grew more authentic, the sound of David felt more like me, and I made the change. Later still, I began using my middle name, Miln, given to me by my parents in honor of A.A. Milne, creator of Winnie-the-Pooh and a relation on my mother's side of the family. As a kid, I didn't like "being related" to Winnie the Pooh, but as an adult, I appreciate my heritage.

Friends may invent nicknames that describe us, and those, too, further shape our self-image in large or subtle ways, depending upon how we feel about the names we are called. *Babe. Tiger. Ace. Fast Eddy. Skinny. Sunshine.* What nicknames did you answer to as a kid?

Women who marry and then divorce have a special challenge and opportunity where names are concerned. Sandra Leicester was born Sandra Jane Lester; when she married, she took her husband's last name. Facing divorce, she realized that reverting back to her "maiden name" felt unsatisfying—that those ten years of learning and growing would be diminished if they weren't honored by a proper new name. Proud of her family line yet wanting her own identity as well, she elected to maintain the sound of "lester" while taking on its centuries-old English spelling.

If we refer to trees, flowers, and animals, we realize that Shakespeare was right. If we call a rose a snowflake, it still blooms in summer, has fragrance, and won't melt. Just the same, words are powerful. A name breathes life into something that before was invisible, ill-defined, or nonexistent. Words point the way to consciousness. What did we do before the word *dysfunctional* appeared in our vocabularies? Or *aerobics*? Or *cyberspace*? Or *personal best*? Or *Hug the Monster*?!

When Jesus chose the Twelve Apostles, he gave each of them a new name. In the Hindu religion, initiates receive a spiritual name as well. Richard Alpert, the Harvard psychologist who later took the name, Ram Dass, often expressed this wonderful irony: "Words exist because of their meanings. Once you've got the meanings, you can forget the words. Where is the person who has forgotten words, so that I may have a word with him?" When we feel a strong connection with someone, we sometimes long to communicate directly, without the burden or inaccuracy of words.

We can discover who we are by the experiences we have. Yet even experiences don't define us. We define ourselves. How many words are there to define you?

How to do A Rose by Any Other Name

Part One: Compare notes.

Fill a page with words that describe you. Then, ask someone else to do the same thing. The distance between how others view us and how we view ourselves is a fascinating journey to travel. Try it.

Part Two: Change your name for one week.

Tell everyone at home and at work what your new name is, and explain that it is a *Hug the Monster* exercise. You may even start a fad in the office. Many people have wondered what it would be like to be called something else. Lee Anne wants to be Lindsay. Ralph would rather be Roger. Notice how it feels to answer to a new set of vowels and consonants. Go for something beautiful, or strong, or lyrical. See what effects it may have on your self-image.

> *The Eskimo has fifty-two names for snow because it is important to them; there ought to be as many for love.*
> —Margaret Atwood

Exercise 10. *Surprise Yourself*
Monster: Being Rigid

When on the Nile, do as the Nubians do" was my passport to a memorable dining experience. I found myself squatting in a mud hut, scooping up food with my right hand out of the same large serving bowl as my six Nubian companions. Exposure to other cultures around the world is a fascinating reality check. It not only pushes our comfort zones, it can actually stir up our equilibrium, too. In Turkey, a nod of the head up actually means "no" rather than "yes." Eating full meals with the right hand is customary in many places—India, Morocco, Tibet, and Nepal, to name a few. If you've ever visited Great Britain, you know that getting behind the steering wheel of a car in England and driving on the left side of the road is a quick way to realize how relative our customs, habits, and daily realities are. And as a pedestrian in London, if you look the "wrong" way before crossing the street, you may find yourself in the path of an oncoming car or bus.

Breaking patterns, climbing out of ruts, and claiming more joy in life means finding out where we are possibly stuck in our ways because of how we've distinguished the "right way" to do things from the "wrong way." Shocking your nervous system by temporarily reversing certain behaviors can be an entertaining wake-up call to other beliefs and habits we have. Learning to make changes in our lives with the greatest ease comes from an insatiable curiosity and passion about life. What begins as a productive routine or a time-saving convenience, such as always shopping at the same neighborhood grocery store, may also be defining your world too narrowly. Surprising ourselves can be fun. To do it, I think we have to be willing to expose ourselves to more of the world now and then with behavior that is contrary to our normal routines. Oscar Wilde said it best: "Consistency is the last refuge of the unimaginative."

How to do Surprise Yourself

Whatever you *always* do, do it another way. Be contrary for a day and see how many times you can surprise yourself. If you need help picturing this, just ask a teenager. They are quite gifted in contrary behavior! Here are some easy and fairly common examples, but make sure you find some that are unique to your own daily routines and habits, too. Switch your hand dominance—if you are right-handed, become a lefty . . . and schedule a round of golf or a few sets of tennis using your other hand! Wear your watch on the opposite wrist and notice how many times during the day you habitually look at your naked wrist-bone expecting to see what time it is. Sleep on the other side of the bed. Write, answer the phone, comb your hair, and brush your teeth opposite your regular patterns. Physically, see how many ways you can perform daily tasks contrary to your norm.

(Here's one you can do right this second. Cross your arms over your chest. Now, without thinking or looking at your arms, recross them, putting the other arm on top. Tricky, huh? Try it another way. Clasp your hands and fingers together. Now repeat it, this time put the other thumb on top. Could you do both ways easily without hesitating?)

Once you're in the swing of things, get imaginative! Say hello when you mean good-bye. Eat dessert first. Do the dishes by hand instead of using the automatic dishwasher. Or use paper plates. Cook over an open flame instead of with the microwave. Have tea instead of coffee. If you live on the north side of town, shop on the south side. Sleep during the day and work alone all night. If you always wake up at 7:15, make it 5:17. If you always wear a tie, don't. Listen to rap instead of classical music. Put an outfit together using your least favorite color and your most comfortable shoes. Pay cash. If you are normally shy, talk to every stranger you meet. Hire a limo to take you to work. Got it? Now go for it! Loosen up.

> *"To live is so startling it leaves little time for*
> *anything else."* —Emily Dickinson

Exercise 11. Ask for Help
Monster: False Pride

I used to think I had to do everything myself until I learned the value of the lesson in this exercise. I came to realize that no matter what mode I happened to be operating in—father, adventurer, corporate speaker, or world traveler—I would gain and grow in thousands of ways simply by asking for help, *once I learned to get the focus off of me and onto the fact that the helpers are there for their own reasons.* New friends, skills, insights, a delicious meal, or a pleasant conversation are just a few of the add-ons you get by putting your pride aside and creating a team. Even more important than the unanticipated bonuses is the fact that you can accomplish more in a group than by acting alone. In order to become a better speaker, I have to constantly put my ego aside and ask for constructive criticism from other professional speakers, from my clients, and from speaking coaches.

Our egos are tender. Asking for help is very frightening for some of us, especially if we're the parent, expert, or boss, believing we should know the answers all of the time. The popular phrase "fake it till you make it" works in some instances, but not in all! Faking it could cost you, your family, or your company precious time, resources, and opportunities.

I'm talking about an attitude here—a state of mind in which you are open to whatever your world has to offer you. It's a willingness to listen and to learn. Sometimes it is a direct request for help. But there are other times, if you are available to be assisted, when the help shows up in synchronicities, perfect timing, and easy problem solving where everything comes together with almost no effort. Asking for help is a great way to go through life, and dispels the mean illusion that people are only out for themselves. Asking for help practically assures an optimistic state of mind all of the time. Who loves a know-it-all? Nobody. People respond with warmth, smiles, and open hearts when we are big enough to admit we don't always know all of the answers.

How to do Ask for Help

Part One: The small stuff.

For one solid week, no matter what you are doing, say to yourself, "How could this be better?" or, "How could this problem get solved by asking for a little help?" Even in your area of expertise, be open to new ideas, improvements, and assistance. Keep track of what happens. Get creative and generous with thank-yous by letting the other person know specifically how they were helpful. Send a postcard, tack a Post-it note to their computer screen, give a granola bar or pack of gum, leave a funny or thoughtful message on someone's voice mail. "Please" and "thank you." What a wonderful concept.

Part Two: Bigger stuff.

Next, set the goal of asking for help three times a day for a week. Be awake to what happens in your body, your head, and your heart. How does it feel? In part one, you tackled little projects for the first few days. Now it is time to move on to bigger concerns and fears. Afraid of flying? Scared to ask for a raise? Hate the thought of confronting your neighbor about the dog droppings in your yard? Instead of getting defensive, ask for support. Make a note of relationships that alter because of it, new friends, and deeper insights you gain along the way. Finally, promise yourself that you'll integrate this attitude into the very fiber of your daily life. People will wonder what's happened inside, and they'll smile at you a lot more often.

Only connect.
—E. M. Forster

Chapter Four

The Logic Monsters

Logic Monsters make a lot of unpleasant noise. They roar and mutter admonitions like "You can't do that!" Or they reprimand us with, "Other people are more creative. Let them be in charge of coming up with the idea for this project." They are known to plop themselves down right in front of us, cross their arms, and scold us mercilessly for acting on a hunch. They don't believe in play, self-expression, or intuition. They are tough little creatures who specialize in "reality" defined by what you can see, touch, taste, hear, and smell. They live in your head, have little or no contact with feelings in your heart or gut, and get most of their power from *thinking*. They scorn those who beat the odds by taking risks, and would rather build fences than blaze new trails. They are sometimes tight with money, are often conversant in all of the bad news of the day, and love to follow rules someone else invented. They bow at the altar of someone else's authority, and get really uncomfortable with questions.

To invite your Logic Monsters to step forward, just ask two of the most important questions in the world, "Why?" and "Why not?" Logic involves a linear process, but much of life experience can't be squeezed and fit into neat little packages, systems, and formulas, try as we might. Logic Monsters are meant to be hugged. Like all the other monsters, to be hugged is the very reason they exist.

By the time we reach adulthood, our creativity and sense of playfulness is often buried deep within us. Consequently, we adopt a perception about ourselves that we aren't capable of artistry, inventiveness, or self-expression. As time passes, we become so invested in that identity, acting otherwise feels terribly risky. When taken to its extreme, we actually avoid having fun. These exercises are for getting in touch with a lighter side of life where our true spirit may be waiting to awaken the visionary within who can write, paint, sing, sculpt, dance, tell stories, act on intuition, and love ourselves unconditionally. Truly authentic, creative acts are life-giving, and often life-saving. Hugging the Inertia Monsters may get us moving, but to stay loose and flexible in the ways we move, we need to hug the Logic Monsters every chance we get.

During the decade of the '80s, much was written about right brain and left brain modes of behavior. The right brain hemisphere offers us creativity and access to our imaginations, and the left brain hemisphere is said to be the home of logic and order. Although simplistic, if this is indeed true, then the Logic Monsters are extremely left-brained creatures who thrive inside us when we don't use our imagination, or worse yet, claim to have none at all. They convince us that reality is defined only by what we can rationally prove and recite facts about. They almost never take risks. Rarely do they giggle, act silly, or break patterns, preferring security to exhilaration.

If you believe only what you can see, touch, hear, smell, taste, or measure, then you've bought into what Deepak Chopra has named "the myth of rational materialism"—a belief system that feels like an exacting scientific method, and in the process, doesn't recognize or account for the mystery or joy of human experience. Some of the highest states of being are impossible to describe, let alone point to with any material proof. *Love* is the emotion of connection. *Peace* is the state of balance and rest for the soul. *Beauty* has a feeling of resonance with truth. *Truth* is a stirring recognition of *what is*. See what I mean? None of those precious words and the states of being they represent can be measured, proved, or defined in any fully satisfactory way. They are *experiences.*

Logic Monsters often pop up when our egos are in conflict with our spirits, when we'd rather defend ourselves than admit we are wrong. If we pay close attention, hugging them automatically produces the wonderful feeling of being alive. If there is a single edict for these exercises, it's this: *Grow and have fun!*

Exercise 12. Abracadabra, It's Magic!
Monster: Illusions

Outside a temple on a dusty crowded street in New Delhi, I met a man who said he could tell my future. I wasn't particularly interested in his offer, but he stopped me in my tracks when he said he had written down the name of my father on a piece of paper, and would show it to me for a price. Now I was fascinated. Since my father's name was an uncommon one, Seymour, I agreed to play along, and sure enough, there it was on the paper! I caught up with my wife and an Indian friend. "Hey, did you tell this guy my father's name?" I asked them. When they said they hadn't, I accepted the feat at face value. I really believed he had read my mind.

A few years later, I met The Amazing Randi, a professional magician, who explained that it was only a trick. According to him, a small piece of pencil lead underneath the seer's thumbnail rapidly scribbled "Seymour" during the moment I was asked to verify the name on the paper. As I spoke the word, he was able to divert my attention and write it down without the motion being detected. The thrill of having had my mind read turned quickly to respect for the trick and the trickster. To this day I really don't know the truth, but learning that it could be done successfully without psychic powers seemed an important awareness. I was willing to consider all possibilities, rather than investing in one only.

Truth and illusion are intimately connected with hugging the monsters we fear. What you see is often not what you get, and vice versa. Superstitions might keep you safe, but they also might keep you from experiencing a fuller life. To discover more truth, we have to peel away illusions as we come upon them, scrutinize them, and cast off beliefs that needlessly limit us. Don't worry, though. There's plenty of real magic in life itself. You won't be bankrupted by piercing the illusions you live with. Indeed, you'll more likely be wealthy in wisdom and self-confidence by what you discover, and perhaps even humbled by what you truly cannot explain in words or with facts.

How to do Abracadabra, It's Magic!

Part One: Learn a magic trick.

Go to a store where they sell magic tricks and purchase three. Learn how to perform them flawlessly for friends, family, and colleagues. You'll always have these little tricks to perform at parties, and you'll have fun insights into what makes David Copperfield and The Amazing Randi have such fascinating, successful careers. Let your new trick become a metaphor for the power of illusion. The Wizard of Oz was just a nice guy from Kansas standing behind a curtain, remember? According to him, "know I'm a very good man. I'm just a very bad wizard." Realizing this allowed Dorothy, the Tin Man, the Scarecrow, and the Lion to grow and get on with their lives. Until that moment, they were stuck. Similarly, when Darth Vader's identity as Luke Skywalker's father became clear, all was well in the universe. Don't be afraid. Pierce your illusions. Hug the monster. *And may the force be with you.*

Part Two. Identify and test the beliefs and superstitions in your life.

Select an idea that is sacred to you and find out if it is really true.

Christopher Columbus in fact didn't sail off the end of a world everyone else believed to be flat. He "discovered" the New World instead. An experience of inner expansion comes with growth. But to grow, we have to be willing to name the illusions we live with. Quantum physics reminds us that the world we perceive with our senses is a very limited view, and that solid matter is really filled with space and energy. Who and what are the authorities in your life? What beliefs are operating in your life that could be called into question? Wherever you encounter the same problem again and again, chances are there is a faulty premise underneath it asking to be examined. We talk a lot about unanswered questions. *What about unquestioned answers?* Examine them for what you know to be real and true *based on your own experience*, and for what you've taken simply on faith. Put them to a test. These could include anything from your ritual of wearing your lucky tie or dress before a big presentation, to your ideas about money, virtue, or religious beliefs and practices.

> *If I am to die in battle, please don't let me die bewildered.*
> —King Arthur to Merlin, *Camelot*

Exercise 13. Be an Animal
Monster: Arrogance

If anthropologists are to be believed, human high-speed, bipedal motion—running—began in East Africa. As an adventure runner, I wanted to experience how First Man roamed, hunted, and was hunted in this timeless and majestic land. As in any adventure, my advance research had to do with the people, their culture, and the terrain. In this case I also read about the animals in a book called *A Season on the Plains* by Franklin Russell, with whom I eventually wrote a book. Growth comes from looking at life from a different perspective. In Russell's African book the main characters were an old male lion who had been kicked out of the pride, a one-eyed female hyena, a leopard, and a baboon. In a meeting with Joy Adamson, author of *Born Free*, I learned that I had to develop a certain connection with the bush animals who might otherwise have me for dinner.

Undoubtedly I was a bit arrogant because I thought I fully understood what she meant. . . .

I realized in the beginning of my first solo run, pretending to be First Man, that I was running in a zoo without fences. My support vehicle dropped me off to run the four miles alone back to camp. Name a wild carnivore and it was nearby—lions, leopards, and cheetahs among them, along with herbivores of tremendous size and power—cape buffaloes, elephants, and rhinos. I felt the full force of genuine, life-threatening fear. Searching for a way out, "I'll climb a tree," I thought. "So can the cats," I immediately answered myself. "Then I'll just swim back," I decided, running to the overlook of the river that flowed down to our campsite. Dozens of crocodiles laced the riverbanks and families of hippos bathed leisurely. Swimming was not an option. A group of gazelles or antelopes ran at an angle toward me, begging the question, "What could be chasing them?" I spotted a troop of baboons two hundred meters in front of me. They walked slowly into the bush. My mind went straight to the fact that with their large, sharp teeth, in a group they can rip and kill a leopard. I sized up the situation. "That's a group." I was trapped and in very serious trouble.

Feeling the sweat dripping from my body, I wondered, "Can the baboons sense my fear?" I heard my mother's voice telling a six-year-old version of myself, "Don't show your fear to dogs." So I slowed my pace to a leisurely stroll, pretending to be cool and calm, and hoping they would buy my act. The outrageous charade made me laugh at myself, and with my sense of humor somewhat restored, I relaxed a bit and began taking in the information around me in a new way. The baboons had entered a cluster of trees. Their lively eyes sparkled at me through the lush leaves and branches as I passed by them. This time, instead of vicious predators, I perceived them as a life-size version of that wonderfully famous Rousseau painting, and realized that a healthy mutual curiosity was the main dynamic operating between us, and nothing more. I was a visitor in their land, and thankfully, they allowed me to tour it unharmed.

I finished my run with most of my fear replaced by awe and respect, having learned far more as "First Man" than I ever expected. We call the wild animals "beasts." I had expected they would be running around eating each other. Not so. I learned that most of them only hunt and eat when they are hungry. Between meals they looked contented, alert, and relaxed. The baboons chattered. Maybe they were laughing at me. I was surely laughing at myself for blowing the fear way out of proportion, remembering my definion of fear: False Evidence Appearing Real.

Arrogance means we are poised at the top of some invisible hierarchy looking down, out of balance with ourselves and our world. Empathy, useful in almost every endeavor, comes quickly when relating to animals. There are times in life when getting a new perspective on problems, opportunities, and challenges is a simple matter of using our imagination in a new way, extending it in empathy with members of the animal kingdom with whom we share this beautiful planet Earth. The wisdom of nature is a kind and patient teacher if we take the time to listen.

How to do Be an Animal

Part One: Become your favorite pet.

If your exposure to animals is limited to cats, dogs, and hamsters, it is enough to begin this exercise. Get down on the ground, or on the back of the sofa, and imagine the view from your cat's perspective. Your dog's senses of hearing and smell are far keener than your own. What sounds and scents can you focus on if you imagine being your dog? What might you learn by getting down on all fours and lapping up water with your tongue? Think about all the creatures you've had some contact with—turtles, frogs, bunny rabbits, birds, squirrels. Study how they walk, sleep, eat, drink, sit, and run. Nature has given each animal everything it needs to cope with the world around it. Observe the wildlife in your world and actively wonder what it is like to be an animal.

Part Two: Select an animal totem.

In Native American lore, one who perceives from less than the Four Great Directions will remain a partial human: Buffalo symbolizes wisdom. Mouse represents innocence and trust. Bear stands for introspection. And the eagle invites illumination and visionary thinking. In many cultures, selected animals are sacred, and a personal totem is assigned to children as they reach puberty as a symbol of their own life path and the protection, attributes, and skills that animal will provide. Imagine what your personal totem might be: a giraffe, a mountain lion, an elephant? Choose an animal that you feel a connection with and learn all about it. For a solid week, let that animal be your "other eyes" and see life in new ways.

Part Three: Walk in someone else's shoes for a day.

Apply what you've learned in parts one and two to your human world. How do we show arrogance in our family life. In the workplace? If you imagine what it is like to be your partner, your assistant, or your child, can you appreciate them in a new way? What talents or wisdom has nature given them to share with you that you may have missed up to now? Perhaps you will gain a new appreciation for the possibility that we are all teachers and all students for one another, that perhaps nature intended it all to work together exactly in this way . . . and that arrogance is another word for ignorance.

> *In a world older and more complete than ours they move*
> *finished and complete, gifted with extensions of the senses*
> *we have lost or never attained, living by voices we shall*
> *never hear.* —Henry Beston

Exercise 14. Direct and Produce
Monster: Creativity

My adventures have been reported as news stories in print and broadcast media, and my photos tell stories that no words can convey. As a speaker, my primary marketing tool is a demo video for prospective clients containing a sample of my work and my message. Ultimately, though, I have film, video, and still-photo records of my life for my own enjoyment, and for those people I love with whom I have shared various chapters of my life. Film and still photography are both professional tools and enjoyable hobbies for me. My house is brimming with audio- and videocassettes, boxes of slides, film cans—some material fully scripted, some spontaneous, all of varying degrees of quality. Recording life events not only preserves them, but adds an urgency to make today even more wonderful than yesterday.

Technology continues to make it easier for novice video-

graphers to have the experience of producing art, enter-
tainment, and personal documentary. Not only video cameras, but also simple editing devices can be rented,
allowing us to keep vibrant records of our lives as we
videotape Little League games, birthday parties, and wed-
dings. While the "special occasions" call out all the cameras, the real meaning in life is found in daily living.
Recording the sights and sounds of today, what would
your movie look like?

How to do Direct and Produce

Haul out your director's chair and a clipboard. You are
going to create a video. The process has many interesting
and fun steps, so take your time. Lack of experience
shouldn't stop you, so move through that easy excuse right
now. If the unexamined life is not worth living, as Plato observed, then it must also be true that the unlived life isn't
worth examining. Dig right in. What will your video be
about? How to make a perfect apple pie? A metaphysical or
spiritual insight you are exploring? Interviews with your
family and neighbors? A project you are charged with at
work? Visual poetry? A music video? Perhaps it's a simple
"day in the life" of someone you admire. The possibilities
are virtually endless. While I've outlined three action steps
in this exercise, be sure you use the five-part method for
hugging the creativity monster: gather information, set the
date, develop the skill, shoot and edit the video, and reflect
on the total experience. Here are some suggestions.

Step One: Select an idea for development.

Consider documenting the way you and others hug
monsters. Make plenty of notes. You'll need a shooting

script, a main character and/or idea, and some sense of the story arc—a beginning, middle, and end. If you want to learn the art of making movies, go to the library and read up on it, or attend a class at your local community college. Things to think about: narration, background music, locations, willing participants, and where to rent a camera and recorder with simple editing capabilities.

Step Two: Shoot and edit the video.

Learn enough about new cameras and proper lighting to make sure your efforts aren't lost due to poor technique. Practice using the camera at different angles, light levels, and distances to learn the power of a spontaneous close-up and the purpose of a panoramic long view. Shoot with editing in mind. Discover the technique and art of story-telling with videotape and savor the spirit in life that is uniquely yours.

Step Three: Show it to someone.

Finally, once it is edited, give copies to friends, mail it to Oprah, or hold a screening in your home, complete with popcorn and reviewers. Perhaps you've created an editorial fit for sending to CBS's *60 Minutes*. If it is humorous, why not send it off to the TV program *America's Funniest Home Videos*? Whatever you do, don't hold back. Go for it. Oh, and send us a copy, too.

> *All real living is meeting.*
> —Martin Buber

Exercise 15. Your Own Wall of Fame
Monster: Lack of Inspiration

The walls of my home are like photo trophy cases—displaying moments, people, and places that I especially treasure and want to remember often. Many of them are small moments and simple acts. Yet they inspire me to live each day to the fullest, taking nothing for granted and affirming that at any point, life is precious enough to warrant a snapshot or two. Photography is a creative, rewarding, and fairly easy way to connect with people, the environment, animals, and meaningful insights.

What makes a great photograph great? I have learned it is not technique and a great camera alone, but also some sense of truth captured in the moment, seen from behind the lens. The photographer must have a sense of purpose and an inspiration before clicking the shutter. She must also be able to stand back from the action and be totally objective in order to see something utterly clearly from behind the lens alone. Boldness is required for exciting close-ups where tighter composition means the possibility of momentarily intruding on someone else. In my experience, though, people are more often tolerant and willing to be photographed than not.

How to do Create Your Own Wall of Fame

Part One: Do it for yourself.

Replace or add to some of your expensive or inexpensive artwork in an area of your home with scenes from your own life. Take a camera to work, to the market, to your favorite parks, rivers, and lakes. Is there an interesting face and story behind the counter at your dry cleaners, health club, or beauty salon? If you were a great photographer like Richard Avedon, Annie Leibovitz, or Ansel Adams, what would you see in your world that you don't see now? Begin seeing your world as if through the eye of a camera. Capture something so interesting and beautiful that you want to frame it and display it.

Part Two: Do it for others.

Take shots with the idea of making holiday and birthday gifts for family members, friends, and coworkers. Use your best photographs to create a twelve-month calendar. Many gift catalogs, photo stores, and copy centers offer such a service these days. Or make a collage with a striking theme. Shoot one roll of film—twenty four or thirty-six exposures—and then make prints of them in all different sizes with the idea of cutting and pasting together a work of art on a particular idea.

In this exercise, as well as exercise 14, follow the five-step method for hugging monsters and you won't find yourself doing the procrastination thing that sneaks in and steals your fun. Gather information, set a date, develop your skill, shoot the photos, and then reflect upon the experience for new meanings and insights. You can grow from this in amazing ways.

> *That's what learning is. You suddenly understand*
> *something you've understood all your life, but in*
> *a new way.*   —Doris Lessing

Exercise 16. Author, Author!
Monster: Self-Expression

Travel has been a major part of my life, but some trips are more memorable than others because of the creativity that was invited to come along. When my son and daughter, Daren and Chelsea, were eleven and eight years old respectively, we went to Marrakech for New Year's Eve. We brought along an audiotape recording of the Crosby, Stills, and Nash song "Marrakech Express" as a kind of sound track to our trip. Once in Marrakech, we purchased Moroccan music, too. Playfully, Chelsea donned a veil and Daren a turban to go exploring the alleylike streets in Tangier. During our little adventure we came up with the idea to write a song about what it was like "sneaking and peeking" our way through the maze of narrow streets. In more recent years, a trip to Costa Rica was made more memorable by writing new words to the tune "Oklahoma!" (selected in honor of the fact that Chelsea was a cast member of her high school's production of the musical that same month), with each verse describing our hotels, the warm ocean, and the magnificent rain forest rivers on which we rafted and kayaked. Now when we sing it, the memories come back larger than life, and our laughter comes easily, too.

I often lead team-building sessions for corporate executives in which a variety of timed games test their creativity, playfulness, and communication skills. The games always culminate with a general debriefing session during which each team reports to the others what they learned. One especially memorable presentation came from a team that wrote and performed an original song about the day's events and their experiences together. As a show-and-tell approach, the singing report was an effective, entertaining way to demonstrate that all three goals—creativity, playfulness, and communication—had been met successfully.

Playfulness can invite creativity in a way that minimizes self-consciousness or shyness. When the only point is to find a new way to love the moment and everyone in it, words and music are a great tribute. But to restrict yourself to music isn't necessary. Writing words to a well-known tune is just the start of possibilities. Greeting card companies have figured this out, too. These days not only are there endless selections of great cards that are blank on the inside so we can express ourselves instead of using another's words, but digital technology has made it possible to offer cards on which our own voices carry loving or humorous messages, or on which we write and design our own greeting with a type style we like.

Many people like to remember events with a favorite line from a movie or a poem. I wonder how many times "Here's looking at you, kid," "May the Force be with you," or "Toto, I don't think we're in Kansas anymore," has been recalled to help punctuate a moment. Thoreau may come to mind as you enjoy the serenity of an autumn day strolling by a lake in the country. People in love quote Shakespeare, Keats, or Elizabeth Barrett Browning to help express the irrepressible urge to speak from the heart. The world is full of artists' treasures for the rest of us to enjoy. How often do you call upon them to frame or underscore events in your life? Have you ever considered taking literary license and doing your own version of your favorite song or poem?

How to do Author, Author!

Part One: Memorize, recite, share.

Everyone has a favorite poem from which they can quote a line or two. Find yours and commit it to memory.

All of it. If the inspiration is about another person, recite it to them. If it is about a place, go to that place and speak it out loud word for word. Is it a moment from the past you want to frame and keep forever? Select the musical or literary work and share it with those who are part of the memory.

Part Two: Put it to music.

Select an event in your life or a scenario that you can put to words and music. Choose a tune that is easy to sing and write new words to it. It could be about your family vacation, a tough project you and your team made it through successfully at work, or merely the way your heart feels about your life right now. Once you've put it all together, perform it. Then put it in your scrapbook, or post it on the refrigerator or bulletin board where you'll see it regularly for a while.

> *Make voyages. Attempt them. There's nothing else.*
> —Tennessee Williams

Exercise 17. Get Crafty
Monster: Apathy

Growing up as a boy involved in all kinds of sports, I didn't relate to the concept or the word *creative*. Although I was innovative in some of the projects I put together in school, I didn't recognize or define myself as that type of person. I believed being creative was for artists and actors. Or even for sissies. Of course, I grew up and got it straight. Creativity is an essential part of what it means to be a human being. The more I realized my own creative nature, the more inventive my adventures became, showing me how to connect continents by swimming between them, for example. My inner growth was enhanced and my life took on greater possibilities as I came to understand the nature of the creative act. Then I couldn't get enough of it. I spent countless hours at the Museum of Modern Art in New York City. I took up oil painting and filmmaking. I took classes at the Brooklyn Museum in welding, jewelry making, clay sculpting, and wood carving. I carved a throwing club that I eventually took to East Africa with the intention of giving it to a Masai warrior. But when I saw the clubs they made, I felt my rendition was so inferior I was unable to give it away. (Regrettably, this is an instance where I gathered information, developed a skill, and set the date, but I didn't actually *Hug the Monster*.)

Peter Drucker, a highly respected business consultant and author of dozens of business books, said he really always wanted to write fiction. In his early seventies, he finally did it. I have a beautiful coffee table book, *Actors As Artists*, by Jim McMullan and Dick Gautier, that features the artwork of film, television, and theater celebrities. What have you always wanted to try? Is there a sketch artist in you as evidenced by doodling on napkins at your favorite café, or on notepads near the telephone? Do you still have the urge to be an actor or actress, although you haven't explored theater since college? Do you look at other people's handiwork such as needlepoint or knitting and wonder if you could produce items of similar beauty and quality? As you sing in the shower do you wonder if you really could qualify for the all-city choir and their annual holiday performance of Handle's *Messiah*? Get ready. Your moment has arrived.

Ignoring or neglecting our creative spirits carries a high price, deeply affecting our view of what's possible in life.

When we don't call upon our own creative reserves, we tend to rely on getting answers from other people. Instead of finding solutions within ourselves, we expect someone else to be the authority. Eventually we stop asking questions of all kinds, and this is certain death to our formerly willing, adventurous spirits. In an information age where experts and authorities abound, this is a particularly important thing to pay attention to. The creative urge is like a pilot light that feeds a flame inside us that grows brighter, warmer, and more important as it gets attended to. Merely thinking about taking action isn't enough. And judging the outcome isn't all that important, either. So what if you don't become a star, rich, or famous? Or your charcoal sketches don't win a blue ribbon when you enter them in the state fair? Stay in touch with the process of creation, not with its result.

How to do Get Crafty

Instructions for this exercise are obvious and direct. Choose the thing you've always wanted to do, and do it. Remember the five steps involved, though. Select your art or craft. Gather information about classes at your local craft store or community college. Find out what you need, what it will cost, and how much time you will need to devote in order to achieve the goal. Hugging this monster involves a finished product to give away or perform. You must actually sing in the choir, frame your artwork, get cast in a play, cuddle up with the afghan you knitted, or write that short story and get it published somewhere. Be patient, do all the steps, and you'll succeed.

> *You are led through your lifetime by the inner*
> *learning creature, the playful spiritual being that is*
> *your real self.*   —Richard Bach, *Illusions*

Exercise 18. Play Follow the Leader
Monster: Low Sights

One of the most colorful individuals I've ever known about is Sir Richard Burton, a nineteenth-century English explorer who completely embodied the definition of Renaissance man. Although best remembered as one who conducted a heroic search for the source of the Nile, his accomplishments are much broader and far more incredible than that alone. He was an author and a geographer. He spoke twenty-three languages and fifty-six dialects. He translated into English *The Arabian Knights* as well as the Indian book of lovemaking, *The Kama Sutra*. In India, he studied to become a Brahmin. He infiltrated the inner circle at Mecca, a holy place from which non-Muslims are barred on threat of death, by artfully and skillfully taking on the mannerisms, dialects, and disguises necessary to be successful. Although I was already an adventurer when I first learned about him, he inspired me in many ways, and is probably the reason I wanted to kayak the Nile, and also to acquire my own Brahmin's string in India.

Though childhood is typically the time when we focus our sights on larger-than-life characters to fuel our imaginations and shape our values, it is never too late to invite heroes and heroines to nourish us with their vision and inform our lives with their courage. Some stories are legendary. Beethoven's deafness. Walt Disney's bankruptcy. Wilma Rudolf's childhood polio. Colonel Sanders was sixty-five and virtually penniless when he invented Kentucky Fried Chicken. Hewlett-Packard was begun in a garage. And while Hollywood and professional sports produce celebrities, genuine role models are plentiful in history books as well as in our own neighborhoods. They are everywhere we find problems, challenges, and obstacles, and the people who vow to overcome them.

When we begin to feel stifled by the status quo in our lives, when our imaginations are dormant and dull, when cynicism has crept into our outlooks, that's the time to go on an all-out search for someone to pull us up to new levels of performance and service.

How to do Play Follow the Leader

Part One: Whom have you long admired?

Perhaps there will be several people on your list. Select one. What do you actually know about that person? Imagine you are an investigative reporter in search of a story. Learn as much as you can about who they are, how they lived their lives, and the obstacles they encountered along the way. Who or what motivated them? Who were their parents? How many times did they "fail" before they succeeded? Become an expert on this person's life and begin to apply the lessons to your own.

Part Two: Now turn the tables on yourself.

Have you ever considered the possibility that you are the hero in your own life? Where have major influences come from? Authors? Family members? Coworkers? Teachers? Circumstances such as physical disabilities or economic hardships? If someone were to interview you, what acts would you tell them about that might offer inspiration to someone else?

Part Three: Refer to the list of dreams you created
in the first warm-up exercise.

What type of hero or heroine could be the catalyst to move you in the direction of one of your dreams? Is it a local artist, a community volunteer, an expert, a local business owner? Where in your world do you have access to meeting and getting to know someone who could advise you on launching the dream you've selected? Meet them. Get to know them. Volunteer to work with them. Put your laziness, cynicism, and/or apathy behind you and reach out to someone who has been where you want to go. They'll be flattered and eager to help.

> *Nothing would be done at all if a man waited*
> *until he could do it so well that no one could find*
> *fault with it.* —Cardinal Newman

Exercise 19. *Gather Round the Campfire*
Monster: Low Self-Esteem

Stories make the world go around; they are golden threads that connect us to ourselves, our environment, and each other. In my own life, the meaning of my adventures emerges most clearly as I tell the stories, because I can see who I was before the adventure, who I was during it, and the "who am I now?" that emerged as a result. In *The Power of Myth*, Joseph Campbell achieved worldwide recognition for showing us the value of stories. I have long been an avid fan of Campbell's work. I related heavily to a myth he named "The Hero's Journey" in which *inspiration* leads one into the *unknown* only to return home again and *tell the story*. Briefly, it goes like this. The would-be hero hears a *call to adventure*, answers it, and leaves home on a quest. He enters the belly of the whale, the dragon's lair, or the dark forest and battles the forces of evil. Now successful, he returns home with his symbolic prize—a silver chalice or a

dragon's tooth—and once home, he must do the most exciting work of all. He must integrate his adventure into the fabric of his life, sharing what he has learned with others.

It is our nature to tell stories. Perhaps *in the beginning was
the story,* as prehistoric men and women told one another of
the hunt, of narrowly escaping death, or merely about what
it's like on the other side of the mountain. With fast action,
evil characters, and plenty of danger, the best moment in a
story is the *moment of truth*—the turning point when
courage transcends and transforms fear, and in the process,
transforms lives. I love films of all kinds, but especially
those that elevate the art of storytelling. Remember Dustin
Hoffman in *Little Big Man*? The adventures and misadventures of Hoffman's character were poignantly told in what
I call "first-person hero," replete with the wisdom, humor,
and objectivity that only time and experience can provide.
Sometimes all it takes is the framework of a story to see the
monsters and how we hugged them.

Can anyone remember life before the TV? Although I
don't believe in longing for "the good old days," I do wonder about the richness of the human community before
television when—forgive me if this sounds a little corny—
people gathered to raise barns, make quilts, and tell their
stories as they worked. Theater, film, books, and television
do certainly expose us to stories, but they rarely ask anything of us, and imply that passive behavior is good
enough. We stop having our own adventures and lose our
ability to appreciate ourselves as heroes and heroines of
our own lives.

How to do Gather Round the Campfire

You are going to hold a storytelling party.

Your guests must arrive prepared to tell a true story about a meaningful experience in their lives. When you send out the invitations, provide everyone with the elements of a great story such as those Joseph Campbell identified as "The Hero's Journey." At the very least, stories need characters, plot conflicts, and resolutions that remind us of human truths and insights. To help people be at ease and understand what is expected of everyone, suggest a time limit of ten minutes per story. When you consider what kind of party you want to have, there are at least two options:

Option One: For self-esteem.

As frames for our personal stories, perhaps the three most important questions in life are "Why me? Why here? Why now?" Answer these at any moment and under any circumstance, and enlightenment is sure to follow. At this party, the stories must be direct personal experiences, but told in "third-person hero" so that your guests can talk about themselves in an objective voice. "She was stuck in a loveless marriage and after years of loneliness and boredom, was resigned to her fate. Then one day . . ." The objective is to frame events that may be common, and transform them into stories of uncommon courage.

Option Two: For inspiring others and building a sense of real community.

To do this version, your guests are instructed to tell someone else's story whom they know personally. Imagine how good it would feel to hear your best friend tell other people about events, traumas, or adventures you've lived, but don't yet see as heroic. For example, volunteering at the AIDS hospice may be just something your friend Steven does easily in the course of his week, but to you it offers tremendous inspiration. Tell Steven's story, and make sure he's at the party to hear it. As you devise the guest list, consider those people with whom you would enjoy a deeper connection, and out of which a real sense of community could emerge.

> *The quest quotient has always excited me more than the intelligence quotient.*   —Eugene Wilson

Exercise 20. It's Impossible
Monster: Questioning Authority

I arrived in Gibraltar to connect the two continents of Europe and Africa by swimming from one shore to the other. I spoke with reporters, lifeguards, swimmers, and even smugglers to gain information about the swim. They all told me the same thing—that it was impossible to swim northward from Africa to Europe. In fact, I sensed they were almost proud of it. "They've all tried it, even your Americans. None have succeeded," the government officials boasted. I learned that it had been attempted seventeen different times in the previous year alone. "But you can see Africa from here!" I kept insisting. Finally, I met with the captain of the *Mons Calpe*, a ship that sailed those waters daily between Tangier and Gibraltar. "I don't know why you blokes come down here for this one. The center current runs into the Mediterranean too swiftly—like a river. She can't be beaten. I even have trouble with it myself some days. It's bloody impossible, and that's it, laddie." The captain was emphatic. They all thought it was impossible—the British, the Gibraltarians, the Spanish, and the Moroccans. Not me. Once I did it, the Gibraltar government considered creating a postage stamp commemorating the feat.

In 1967, two months after I had succeeded at the impossible Africa-to-Europe swim, I went to the English Channel to organize an International Peace Relay team that would break the world record. I wanted to demonstrate what happens when people of different cultures really come together as a team. Our six-member team included men from England, India, Pakistan, and the United States (myself), and women from Canada and Australia. The combination was especially meaningful because India and Pakistan were at war, and the swimmers were officially sponsored by their respective governments—a genuine vote for peace, I thought. Yet when the day arrived for the swim, the Pakistani man dropped off the team, and ironically, his reason had nothing to do with his Indian teammate. As he explained it to me, "In my country, women do nothing on the same level as men. I would be in disgrace when I returned home." Because he was such a fast swimmer, I saw his participation as essential to breaking the record. I was locked into breaking the record, so we canceled the swim. To me, it was impossible to do it without him. Too bad. My mistake.

When I was inspired to trek over the High Atlas Mountains and through the Sahara Desert, I heard similar responses. "It's a hostile place with hostile people. It's impossible to get through it alive," everyone warned. I did it anyway, and the experience was among the most transformative of my entire life. I'd sure hate to have missed it by accepting someone else's fear and beliefs as the whole truth.

These and other experiences of questioning authority have transformed my outlook on life. I am an advocate for the impossible. *Why is it impossible?* is my favorite question. Yet, doing the impossible to prove a point was rarely, if ever, my sole motivation. Something inside of me called out to have certain experiences, and I learned to honor that voice, my inner self, above all the others. Successfully attempting what *seems* impossible to others, in this sense, is about finding the courage to allow full expression of the true self. In order to do the thing our spirit is asking us to do, we must confront, bypass, or move through the sound logic and good reason of well-intentioned experts, authorities, family members, and friends. We must learn to heed, trust, and nourish the voice inside that *insists it knows otherwise.* The voice gets stronger and clearer with experience. The first time is perhaps the hardest. Do it once, and you'll never be the same again. For added inspiration, realize that every important advance throughout history—in sports, medicine, science, technology, business, the arts, politics— occurred because someone broke through an impossible barrier.

How to do It's Impossible

Step One: What is your heart's desire?

Everyone has a secret question that concerns what might be, or *might have been.* Review your list of dreams from the warm-up exercises. If anything strikes you as impossible, look again. I'm willing to bet that something on that list is sparkling in your mind's eye, speaking to you in a special way. What is it? Why is it impossible? What must you do to begin? Can you use the five-step method, How to Hug a Monster, to begin moving toward it? No matter how long it takes, why not make a commitment right now to do that thing that seems impossible? Don't let your dreams pass you by. Discover what your "two laps" might be in order to one day swim from Africa to Europe.

Step Two: Do a headstand.

This may seem like a nonsequitur, but it isn't. As a metaphor for doing the impossible, it means you will turn yourself upside down and get a perspective that is 180 degrees different from your normal one. In my years as a yoga teacher, I encountered lots of people who "absolutely knew" they couldn't do a headstand *until, working together, I showed them they could.* Since it is one of the most beneficial postures in hatha yoga, I wanted people to get the benefits. *They did.* So, you're next. And by the way, it only looks difficult. Among the health benefits are an increased supply of blood and oxygen to the brain, eyes and ears, a stronger back, and thanks to gravity, stimulation of your entire organ system . . . heart, lungs, stomach, intestines, etc.

Here's how to do a headstand:

1. If you are going to use a wall for support, be sure to clear the area of sharp edges or breakable objects. Use a thin pillow or towel as a cushion for your head. It is best to have a friend to be your spotter the first time you try it.

2. Sitting on your heels facing the wall, place your hands flat on the floor about eighteen inches from the wall and begin to lean forward, putting weight on your hands.

3. You are going to make an equilateral triangle using your hands and the top of your head. Or, imagine your

hands are two points on a tripod, and the top of your head, when placed on the pillow, completes the tripod. Once your hands and head are positioned comfortably for balance, lift your trunk by "walking" slowly on your toes toward the wall.

4. A gentle bounce will lift your feet and legs toward the ceiling. Lift them all the way up, using your spotter and the wall for support.

5. You've got it! Now breathe and count to ten.

6. When you are ready to come back down, tuck your knees into your chest and slowly lower your legs back to the floor. Uncurl slowly and stretch out flat for a moment or two.

And you thought it was impossible. Look at you. You just hugged the monster. Yes!

> *The Nature of This Flower Is to Bloom.*
> —Alice Walker

Exercise 21. *I Have a Hunch*
Monster: Intuition

As a kid growing up in San Francisco, I was an eager competitor partially because those were the values of the times in which I was raised, and also because I was lucky to be born a natural athlete. I loved games and sports of all kinds. I learned to translate the competitive spirit of sports into everything I did, making me a high achiever. In my late teens and early twenties, that spirit manifested itself as bigger mischief, more drinking, and better parties. The shift in orientation from competing with others to competing with myself was a fundamental turning point in my personal growth. But the shift wasn't complete until I discovered an essential nature of my inner life. . . .

Rough-water long-distance swimming, trekking deserts, climbing mountains, and solo wilderness marathon runs challenged and tested my physical endurance and my mental toughness, for sure. During the '60s when I first began having these adventure experiences, psychologists like Carl Rogers, Rollo May, and Abraham Maslow were just beginning to explore new views of human potential. The groundbreaking, experimental work had barely begun at laboratories like SRI International and places like Big Sur's Esalen Institute. Libraries and bookstores were not yet filled like they are today with books urging us onward by directing us inward. The vocabulary of peak performance, flow state, and transformation was little known back then. I certainly didn't have a framework within which to understand what was happening to me every time I went somewhere else in the world and came home significantly changed. Yet, out of my adventure experiences I tapped into something I called *the source*, and from it I began understanding some thing new to me: that challenging myself instead of competing against others was far more rewarding, that noncompetitive sports was a really valid, perhaps revolutionary idea filled with wonderful possibilities.

With a strong hunch that I was onto something, I began talking about this new concept, and created adventures that carried themes of transformation through self-discovery; that pursued personal bests instead of world records. It wasn't a very popular idea at first, especially with coaches I met in schools and debated on national talk shows. My primary point was to encourage all people, not just gifted athletes who could make the team, to involve themselves in sport for fun, fitness, and inner growth. *Sports Illustrated* thought my ideas provocative enough to feature them in a cover story, and perhaps the philosophy helped contribute to the explosion in running and fitness that soon followed throughout our country.

The goal of transformation is discovering a connection with the pure essence inside us that is energetic, loving, wise, compassionate, creative, full of joy, and capable of healing. At the time I was discovering it, I didn't have words or concepts like *mind-body*. Yet the essence of this reality came through. Where did it come from? Considering the competitive values of my childhood, this is especially amazing. My boldness and confidence kept me on the edge in terms of adventure, but my intuition kept me healthy, relatively injury free, and in many instances, alive. Scientifically, we still do not have adequate explanations for intuition and how it functions. Nevertheless, anecdotal material is plentiful. Humans are intuitive—*we can know things*. And when we do, logic is mostly irrelevant because the experience itself is so powerful. I suspect intuition is a function of expanded awareness, of tapping into a source greater than our individual selves, and is an indication of a connectedness we have with all of life.

"I'm not intuitive" may be your current position. Perhaps you'll challenge yourself on that. If you choose not to believe in intuition as a faculty of human awareness, then you may never get to have the experience. But if you make a habit of hugging monsters, pursuing your heart's desire, and testing yourself to your absolute limits, sooner or later the breakthrough will be there. *It will happen*. You'll have a peak experience that changes your ideas about who you really are and what your purpose is in life. You don't have to trek the Sahara solo, jump into the Mayan Well of Sacrifice, or swim from Africa to Europe. That happened to be the way I did it because it was my path. Your path is uniquely yours.

It has been said that hitting bottom can be a peak experience, as well. Getting to a point of no return, of realizing "I can't live like this anymore," is also a turning point many people have in common.

How to do I Have a Hunch

Proposing an exercise for developing intuition is a little tricky, because intuition tends to work differently for everyone. Highly visual people tend to "see" information in their mind's eye. If you are kinesthetic, your body will give you signals and the information will seem to come through your muscles, your stomach, or even your tingling hands or head. Others report hearing information, such as hearing a voice speak.

So the first step in your practice may be to *determine if one of your inner senses is stronger than another.* For example, have you ever known who is on the phone before or as it rings? It's a fairly common manifestation of intuition. If you've had this experience, do you merely think of the person, do you hear their voice, or see their face? This is a simplistic illustration, but hopefully it helps you get the point. Practice "tuning in" to yourself, and see if you can increase the number of times you "guess correctly" who is calling.

Another way to find your intuitive connection is to *pay attention to your dreams* when you sleep at night. Keep a notebook by the bed and jot them down immediately upon awakening. The mere act of turning your awareness inward will encourage an intuitive connection. You may then begin to discover that your dreams contain helpful information and lead you to making important decisions with greater clarity and skill.

Finally, *learning to meditate* facilitates the kind of connection that supports intuitive functioning. You'll find a meditation exercise called Sunrise Sunset in the Eternal Monsters section. Meditation practice is merely the act of physical relaxation combined with mindfulness, but it is something that gets richer with experience. Cultivate it and you'll be glad you did.

> *Problems can not be solved at the same level of consciousness that created them.* —Albert Einstein

The Relationship Monsters

If hugging Inertia Monsters helps us to get moving forward, and Logic Monsters urge us to add dimensions of creativity and play to our lives, then the Relationship Monsters serve us in equally important, yet distinctly different ways. These little rascals pop up every time somebody "pushes your buttons." They tell you when you are in emotional and psychological pain, when your ego is too big or too small, and when getting along with others at close range feels dangerously threatening.

When it comes to close friends, family members, and partners, we tend to believe that the status quo is permanent, that significant personal growth ceases at some magical point in our lives and that "having it all together" is the equivalent of completing a finite checklist. When communication chokes and sputters, when remaining a victim seems justified, when we judge our vulnerability as a weakness, and when isolation is the best solution to a problem, you can be sure the landscape is full of Relationship Monsters begging to be hugged. And if walking away from a relationship is actually the best thing to do, they may keep you from acting on that decision. They thrive on confusion, fuzzy boundaries, competition, and lack of cooperation, and create a stir when self-esteem is especially low. They are overheard expressing many variations on these familiar themes: *How dare you. That's not my job. You always want your own way. But mine is better than yours. I can do it all by myself—I don't need anyone else.* And the all-time winner, *That's just the way I am.* They get terribly excited when we are defensive, too.

One of the truly ironic and frustrating qualities of bona fide Relationship Monsters is that they are quite often transparent and obvious to everyone but ourselves at the time they make an appearance. *In fact, that's their function in life—to help us connect with ourselves and other people precisely when we'd rather not.* They manifest as monsters named boss, parent, child, partner, friend, neighbor, and stranger. It takes plenty of courage to stretch our arms out and hug them. When you get intimate with them, you may discover that they hold many of the keys to your desires, especially the deepest desires of your heart.

Because relationships come in hundreds of shapes and sizes, so do the Relationship Monsters. At intimate, close range is just one spot these critters perform their dance. They also show up in our relationship to the self, and in the way we are citizens in our communities. They teach us that life is interdependent *by design*, and that the "logical, scientific" single-cause-to-single-effect relationship is a narrow, inadequate view of human problems and human possibilities. We learn to understand that each experience enlarges us, and that what happened in the past doesn't necessarily indicate what will happen in the present or future, because we and the people we live with do not stay the same. We are always changing. Every moment holds healing possibilities. They teach us empathy, and why walking in someone else's shoes is the best medicine for healing a hurt or clearing up a misunderstanding.

Another shield that goes up when the Relationship Monsters are present is any form of *us vs. them*, and *me against you*. While the battle is raging, we almost never want the monster to win, because it implies that *we will lose*. But that's exactly how you know one is present. It looks like win/lose, yet win/win is nearly always the final result, even though the shape it takes may surprise you. A stronger sense of self comes from hugging Relationship Monsters. Wisdom, compassion, and humility are their true trademarks, which is why hugging them is an act of self-love, forgiveness, and essential connection. Relationship Monsters are well worth celebrating. In the end, they help us see that even with the dedication and hard work involved in living a full, productive life, there is much joy to be experienced. Having fun and enjoying one another, we can wonder now and then if perhaps *it's all about a party*. Teaching us how to love one another, ourselves, and our world is their only real mission. *What's not to hug?*

Exercise 22. "Do You Know What I Like about You?"
Monster: Vulnerability

Among the hundreds of places I've worked as an adventurer, none is more special to me than Earth House, where I've led over fifty outdoor adventures since 1974. Earth House, located in East Millstone, New Jersey, is a residential alternative treatment center for young adults suffering from major mental disorders, primarily schizophrenia. It's an amazing, wonderful place where the courage to hug monsters takes on a whole new meaning. The staff and patients at Earth House have taught me much over the years about an extraordinary human capacity to embrace fear and express love openly.

Many of the patients at Earth House have a history of suicide attempts. A severe pattern of substance abuse is very common. Most of the patients have never been able to function on their own in the world. Many, if not most, have had multiple diagnoses along with extended hospitalization in attempts to treat and manage their illness. Several times a year, a vanload of schizophrenic patients with diagnoses ranging from mild to severe heads out into the wilderness for four days of unusual therapy—rappelling, hiking, swimming, camping, and outdoor games we call Earth Adventures. On the fourth day, with the bulk of the hard stuff behind us, we play a game called, "Do You Know What I Like About You?" I am always amazed at the transformation I see on the kids' faces. Withdrawn, depressed patients light up. Hyperactive ones calm down. Their private demons silenced for a period, they enjoy rare moments of pure joy. They bond with each other and have genuine, obvious fun giving and receiving compliments—

a rare experience indeed for those who suffer from schizophrenia. If they can do it, anyone can do it.

Natural innocence is worth just about any effort to recapture, and playing this game puts you in touch with a kind of loving innocence that most of us lose by the time we land in first grade and learn about competition. As adults, we have a tendency not to give one another helpful feedback. Yet, when we only do it on special occasions, we reinforce the idea that only special occasions deserve such sharing of insights and compliments. An honest compliment delivered from our heart almost always makes a meaningful connection with another person, whether it's a spouse, partner, or prospective employer. What if it feels too risky to tell these kinds of truths, especially to people we don't know well? There's the monster. Hug it. If you doubt there's a big enough payoff to take the risk, or that you can give sincere compliments to virtual strangers, imagine being on the receiving end of this game and you'll be motivated to try.

How to Play "Do You Know What I Like about You?"

Part One: People you know well.

There are several options for doing this exercise. First, for one week, make a commitment to the phrase "Do you know what I like about you?" as part of your daily routine. Write it down in the places you often look . . . your desk, calendar, car, and/or the bathroom mirror. Say it to three people every day, and keep track of who they are. Start with the people you live with, then expand the exercise to the people you work with. As you are passing out compliments, don't forget to include yourself. Having the kind of awareness that *intends* to compliment means something else, too. This change in awareness or attitude will help you to be an instant optimist if pessimism clouds your outlook from time to time.

Part Two: People you don't know well.

What would life be like if you assaulted your neighbors with nice things to say all of the time? Sincerity is essential, but you may be surprised at how easy it is. For example, to your next door neighbor, you might offer: "Do you know what I like about you? The way you care for your roses. The neighborhood looks so pretty thanks to your green thumb." Or even approach "strangers" such as grocery store baggers, the UPS guy, the Fed Ex lady, letter carriers, and others who deliver necessary services but who remain faceless and nameless all too easily. "Do you know what I like about you? You always put my groceries in thoughtfully so I can easily carry the bags, and you always have something funny to say to me when I shop here. I really appreciate that about you."

Be vulnerable. Be generous. Better yet, be generously vulnerable.

> *There are two ways of spreading light: be the candle or the mirror that reflects it.*   —Edith Wharton

Exercise 23. Play the Fool
Monster: Profound Embarrassment

During my Everyman's Olympics in 1972, one event was to play a storyteller as the Fool in the famous square in Marrakech where snake charmers, scorpion eaters, and other storytellers perform for passersby. It is a fifty-act circus from medieval times. I spread my small rug on the ground as my audience of curious strangers gathered one by one to see what I was up to. Although I couldn't speak their language, I was intent on communicating with them. For a full hour, in story form I pantomimed the events of my Adventure Decathlon, including the story of spending the night in St. Michael's Cave when I scared myself silly and first learned the awareness of hugging monsters. The longer my story went, the more relaxed I became and the more fun I had. I saw that the more I opened up, the more my audience opened up to the story. Finally, they were engaged and applauding. I had won them over. I still feel foolish whenever I watch the film of the experience, and that's okay, too.

In 1970, when *Sports Illustrated* put me on the cover for my view of noncompetitive sports, I was proud and overwhelmed to receive that kind of recognition for my work, especially because it was a big departure from the kind of story they typically reported on the cover. To punctuate it, they declared me a "Super Hippie." Although I would have chosen a different label if it had been up to me, it was their way of calling attention to my new ideas, along with my long hair, suede fringed jacket, and snakeskin boots. That was then, and this is now. I couldn't pass for a hippie if I tried. My hair is short. I wear suits and ties. I'm involved in business and work with *Fortune* 500 companies. Still, my nineteen-year-old son's friends tease me by calling me Super Hippie, and I love it. Why? It is a connection between their world and mine that combines respect and a little bit of humor, too. And I'll take that any day. If you are willing to don the right attitude, there's a lot of residual freedom in playing the Fool.

Warning: This isn't easy, but it is worth doing. In other words, vanity is its own lousy reward. If you value being taken seriously, this one is especially for you. If you fear embarrassment, not knowing, or being judged harshly, this is potent medicine. Our attachments to our identity can melt away with a little effort, freeing us to be more of who we really are.

How to do Play the Fool

Part One: With people you know.

You can do this a number of ways, so take some time to think it through and make a plan. For a friend's birthday, write an original silly song or poem and deliver it like a singing telegram. Be a clown at a child's party. Agree to be the goofiest Santa Claus your office has ever invited to the Christmas party. Dress up as the Easter Bunny and parade around your local mall, telling stories to the kids who gather around you.

Part Two: Public embarrassment.

Invent a character, put on an interesting costume, and hang out by the fountain in the town square at lunchtime, spinning yarns. Or go to a football game with a painted face. Learn how to do mime, and stand by the elevator at work greeting people as they arrive in the morning. Your imagination is your only limit. Go to a costume store and explore your ready-made options if you need some help.

Have fun. Lose control. Above all, get really, really embarrassed.

> *When we see how funny we are, we see how*
> *dear we are.* —Anne Wilson Schaef

Exercise 24. Healing Relationships
Monster: Forgiving and Letting Go

Until my father's near-fatal heart attack, our relationship was constrained and somewhat distant. Like a lot of father/son connections, we didn't easily communicate our feelings to one another. He was strict and expected a lot. He expressed his pride in my achievements to other people, but not to me. I respected him for the intelligent, strong, compassionate physician he was, but for years we didn't enjoy a real friendship. Instead, we argued and debated a lot, and he generally won. His heart attack had been so severe, he was actually dead on arrival at the hospital and suffered broken ribs in the process of being resuscitated. When I saw him lying there, multiple tubes invading his arms, nose, and mouth, I felt he might die without knowing how much I loved him. I spoke the words to him for the first time: "I love you, Dad." Unable to speak, his expression registered a warm response, and he squeezed my hand. In that moment his heart rate increased, setting off a series of alarms, and our private moment was interrupted by emergency nurses. Given his fragile condition, hearing those words nearly killed my father. Thankfully, he fully recovered and lived to practice medicine another ten years. . . . We spent more time together, our relationship soared. . . . We became good friends. And I even won a few debates.

In many of my adventures, something I learned to call my "purity of purpose" has insured my safe passage when it seemed nothing else could. Other people call it a pure intention. It gives me a kind of energy force, and with it comes the sense or feeling that I can totally trust it. From encountering Nubian crocodile hunters and hostile Egyptian fishermen on the Nile to negotiating with a business client, tremendous self-confidence comes from inner clarity and a peaceful mind. When danger, fear, confusion, or pain is lurking, I've learned to check my motives . . . to make sure I am awake to ambiguity, deception, or any other kind of inner conflict. When necessary, I make an adjustment. For example, I may need to move away from a competitive win/lose orientation, to one that is as win/win as possible. Once I'm listening to my heart, peace of mind is easier to achieve and conveying my good intentions comes naturally. *With a peaceful mind, any action tends to be the right action.*

Martial arts such as aikido and tai chi teach a similar concept in the physical realm where the goal involves learning to flow and harmonize with whatever is going on, instead of blocking or fighting. To live in a totally unedited way—to be who you are at all times—requires mindfulness, discipline, and staying in touch with your heart. It also takes a little courage, some skill, and plenty of practice, especially in relationships with those closest to us where things are taken for granted, words go unspoken, and hearts are left to mend on their own.

Deepak Chopra teaches that a self-actualized person is one who can use "the mirror of relationships for their own personal evolution." We take a big chance when we choose to go through life with broken relationships. They fester inside us and become emotional hurdles that can force us to take debilitating detours in other relationships where healing may take years. I'm fairly certain that until we get it right, we'll continue to meet this monster. So why wait if the opportunity is right in front of you? The best approach may be hugging it now, in the very moment conflict pops up. You could fill a dozen libraries with the books that have been written on this subject. Yet, hugging this monster isn't a head trip. Quite the contrary. Analyzing is not the answer. To make it real, you must find your purity of purpose, take the loving action, and not worry about the outcome. It's called *letting go*. Here are some ways to practice letting go.

How to do Healing Relationships

Part One: With yourself.

Do a scan of the people in your life, both past and present, contemplating the question: Where is attention needed? Write down the names and issues that you believe should be resolved. It may be easy to come up with one or two, but don't stop there. Keep going, because you may even find a pattern to your own behavior by the nature of the wounds you detect. A good helping of empathy and intuition is useful here, too, since miscommunication is often at the source of them. For example, how often have you said one thing, and the receiver heard or interpreted an entirely different message? Sometimes the tone of voice we use becomes the message, regardless of the words being spoken. Although it may not be easy, letting go becomes a fairly *simple* thing to do once you've resolved communication issues. In other words, sometimes words just don't come out right, and relationships get snarled and tangled up in the misunderstanding. What you thought was a major disagreement can turn out to be nothing more than poor communication. So, you may want to scan for the little things first. Here's an aspiration in the form of a question that cuts through it for me, and I offer it as a potentially meaningful goal for you as well: *What if we were able to live with the assumption that absolutely everyone we encounter is doing his/her best all of the time?* How would that frame of mind change the way you feel about relationships that need healing?

Part Two: With others.

Select three people with whom you would like to clear the air. Write your thoughts down in a letter for clarity's sake. Perhaps it goes no further. Do you want to take more steps? Then, one at a time, either telephone them or visit them and say what has gone unsaid. Listen to their point of view. Laugh. Share a meal or a moment with them. Thank them for being in your life. Reflect upon the experience afterward and make a new commitment to openness by integrating this practice into your life. You may discover that a former adversary has become a new friend. Or you may confirm what you suspected: that time has passed, things have changed, and the relationship has run its full course. Either way, closure and letting go is a good thing. It is necessary before one can begin again.

> *"I am convinced," Thoreau wrote, "that to maintain one's self on the earth is not a handicap but a pastime—if we live simply and wisely." But Thoreau had no children. He lived alone at Walden Pond. He visited his mother once a week; she did his laundry.*
>
> —Sy Safransky, publisher, *The Sun* magazine

Exercise 25. Getting to Know You
Monster: Making New Friends

In spite of the hassles, traveling in foreign countries is worth it. Some of the most intense travel anywhere is found in India. The Indian tourist board may not be happy about that statement, but it is a fact. In this country that we tend to think of as slow-paced and "laid back," going from one place to the next is often hair-raising. The roads are bad and so are most of the drivers who, without reserve, pass on the wrong side, never stop honking their horns, and swerve without warning to miss any number of cows, oxen, elephants, camels, or people on bicycles with whom they share the roads. Head-on collisions are fairly common. Indian train stations and bus terminals are teeming with people who seem at ease with what looks like organized chaos to foreigners. When Sandy and I traveled in India for six weeks, we did it by auto ricksha, bicycle ricksha, rowboat, airplane, speedboat, taxi, public bus, private car, and train. One train trip was thirty-four hours nonstop.

I was experienced in strenuous, nontraditional travel in third world countries, but this was Sandy's first exposure. I gained additional respect for her and offered my heartfelt applause for the way she repeatedly rose to the occasion in many intense situations. Sharing a place like India together created a bond in our relationship that our daily routines probably couldn't do in a hundred years.

Over the years of sharing adventures with people, I am convinced that one of the best ways to really get to know someone and establish a meaningful bond is to do something totally intense together. Travel is just one way. Camping, kayaking, bike trips, wilderness trekking, and hiking are a few other favorites of mine. But if outdoor pursuits are never going to be your way, there are still plenty of options for creating an intense circumstance to share. The requirements are fairly basic: a common goal or destination that involves stretching your physical, mental, and/or emotional capacities, and enough time to let each other's monsters surface, be identified, and be hugged.

People *move through* our lives. Only a small number of them show up at the beginning and stay until the end. Over the natural course of a lifetime, we're bound to have dozens of special relationships. Yet, unless you are a fortune-teller who can see the future, you don't know how long someone will be in your life, or how long you'll play a significant role in someone else's . . . ten years, or ten days. The best policy, it seems to me, is finding a way to grab the moment and discover one of life's greatest joys: unmistakable, clear, personal connections with others. Often long after your paths have taken you in new, separate directions, the bond remains as vital and nourishing as the moment it was first created. Furthermore, there are no guarantees that these kinds of connections will ever occur. I believe we have to make them happen.

How to do Getting to Know You

You're going to have an adventure with someone. Who you invite and what you do together is completely up to you. Just make sure the activity will be a stretch physically, and completely out of pattern mentally and psychologically with your daily routines and topics of conversation. Walking, biking, hiking, touring, exploring—these are the best. A four-day trip to a big city like New York. A weekend retreat in the mountains. A week-long visit to a health spa in the desert. A full day of exploring the nooks and crannies of your own hometown for little-known bookstores, cafés, and secondhand stores would even suffice. As you consider your adventure, be on the lookout for some of these monsters: Fear of rejection. Of embarrassment. Of not being able to go the distance. Of discomfort. Of more teamwork than you are normally comfortable with. Of giving up control. *So many monsters, so little time.* Bring a camera and plan on a framed photo as a souvenir for you both.

Part One: People close to you now.

Perhaps you'll choose a friend with whom you've had a past misunderstanding and use the time together to invite healing. Or someone in your immediate family—parent, spouse, or child   in order to create a special bond outside of your familiar routines. Take a close look at the important people in your life and imagine what it would be like spending an entire day at the beach together or exploring the trails in a nearby state or national park with no distractions like games, music, or the biggest culprit, work-related talk. *"How would you like to . . . .?"* is always a great opening line if you think the idea may meet with resistance at first. Plan your event, set the date, do whatever preparation is needed, and expect the connection to happen. It will.

Part Two: People you'd like to know better.

Somewhere in your world is an individual you'd like to know better. Perhaps you work together but have never played together. Or perhaps you recently met at a community function. Or the person has been your neighbor for five years and you've only chatted in the driveway. The individual you have in mind could become a mentor, a new best friend, or a lifelong partner. The thing is, you never know at the start. And if you don't take action, perhaps you'll never find out. Pick up the phone and invite him/her to lunch or dinner. Have your plan in mind, and offer the invitation over salad; by the time you get to coffee, your adventure will be hatched. Hold off on dessert. Before you pay the check, set the date . . . and for the best outcome, make sure it is *sooner* rather than later. Your adventure together will be the real dessert.

> *Few people know how to take a walk. The qualifications . . .*
> *are endurance, plain clothes, old shoes, an eye for nature,*
> *good humor, vast curiosity, good speech, good silence, and*
> *nothing too much.*   —Ralph Waldo Emerson

Exercise 26. Do You Think I'm Sexy?
Monster: Bedroom Variety

We'd probably all love to talk about sex more openly if we could figure out how to do it in a way that wasn't potentially embarrassing, disrespectful, or awkward. Do you agree? Locker rooms and beauty salons perhaps still win as the most popular, safest places to discuss and gossip about our "intimacies," although these days I suppose we should add the Internet. In the last thirty years the social sexual pendulum has swung all the way from the free love of the '60s to the safe sex of the '90s. But through all of this, I wonder, are we growing more comfortable making love to each other? Feeling at home in our bodies as sexual beings? Experiencing genuine intimacy? Becoming better, healthier, more well-adjusted people? Being able to sustain committed relationships beyond the exciting, romantic infatuation stage? In light of these questions, *Hug the Monster* would be incomplete without mentioning the subject in a way that examines our fears and how to break through them for a fuller life.

No matter how many ways the pendulum swings, I have the strong impression that the work and the payoff ends up being between ourselves and our partners. I suspect that the ability to enjoy great sex depends upon a willingness to hug monsters that are unique to each of us, our upbringing, prior relationships, and even religious training and moral beliefs. As is true with so many of the other monsters, judging, overanalyzing, and philosophizing won't get us very far at all. We must risk embarrassment, disclosure, our own ignorance, and shyness to find the place in our hearts where we know love is alive and well, and take action. Learning what it means to love ourselves may be the most effective measure we can take in order to find the sexual fulfillment we sense is available to us in a loving relationship.

Perhaps one of the core issues is *experience*. Let's face it. It's a double-edged sword. If we are too experienced, we are judged in a certain, perhaps unfavorable way. And if we are not experienced enough to be comfortable expressing our desires, let alone acting on them, we fear being judged in an equally unfavorable way. Yet, who would disagree about the fact that the human body is a miracle worthy of exploration and celebration? Giving and receiving love through sexual play, tenderness, and passion shouldn't be the source of so many problems or cloaked in such ignorance. Once again I say that hugging monsters is worth it, especially the ones in the bedroom. Here are a few suggestions to help you in hugging this all important Relationship Monster.

How to do Do You Think I'm Sexy?

Part One:

If your partner were a mind reader, what would he or she learn about pleasing you? In other words, do you know what you want? You don't have to talk about it with your partner until you are ready, so the first step is purely to establish clear communication as the goal. Reference great scenes from romantic movies or novels if that helps. Is it difficult for you to use certain words and speak in a sexy way? Practice by replacing euphemisms with precise language. Talk to friends about it. Clip magazine articles and share them with your partner. Read books. Be committed to clarity, getting answers to questions you've wondered about since adolescence, and knowing where you wish to begin. The five step method, How to Hug a Monster, works here, too.

Once you've done the first step, your next one may be to ask the same of your partner. What does your partner really want? What would drive him or her wild? Ask for details and facts. Giggle together, admit your shyness if that's what's going on. *Stay in the moment* during your conversation. If ecstasy were a place, what would it take to go there? When you are both ready, dedicate a day or evening to exploring the issues and experiences that each of you wants to bring to light in the relationship as it relates to problem sex, mediocre sex, great sex, and making love. Talk about your patterns—the ones you especially enjoy, and the ones that could use some variety. Frank conversation may be all it takes to eliminate boredom and increase passion in the bedroom and in the relationship.

Part Two:

If we conducted a survey, we would likely discover that predictability is rarely an aphrodisiac. *Break your patterns.* To be sexy we must feel sexy. Imagine that you are the sexiest love god or goddess on earth. If your sexual relationship needs rekindling because the passion has subsided, making love is routine, or you would merely enjoy some variety, perhaps a little or a lot of imagination is called for. For example—and this is fairly tame—if you make love only at night in the bedroom, do it during the day in the living room. Why not visit an adult bookstore together? Or read adult magazines to each other? Or get a copy of the *Kama Sutra, the Indian Book of Love Making* and explore it together, learning some of the breathing techniques and movements of tantric yoga? Wear provocative clothing reserved only for the two of you. Perhaps redecorating your bedroom is in order, making it more sensual, with soft pillows, interesting lighting, erotic pictures, and spaciousness. How about scattering the love nest with rose petals? Introducing oils and incense into the experience? Or seeing if you can bathe together without having intercourse as a goal, focusing on intimacy, not orgasm? Here's another one: Prepare a special meal full of rich, erotic dishes that tantalize and stimulate the senses, and then feed each other with your hands.

Finally, at the risk of reinforcing stereotypes I'll go out on a limb here and say it for all who already agree: If you are a man, go for more romance and tenderness before, during, and after lovemaking. If you are a woman, take charge.

> *Only the united beat of sex and heart together can*
> *create ecstasy.*   —Anaïs Nin

Exercise 27. We're a Team

Monster: Independence vs. Interdependence

Fortunately, I came to understand early in my career that I couldn't do adventures and expeditions alone, even when the event itself was a solo. From sponsors who provided financing, to teammates who were on the boat looking out for trouble while I battled swells in rough waters, to mentors who offered wise counsel and extra motivation, the support of many people has always provided a critical ingredient to successfully accomplishing the feat. Sometimes such people literally saved my life. In fact, it might be accurate to say *the greater the achievement, the greater the teamwork.* Ask any Oscar winner, CEO, Olympic gold medalist, or best-selling author.

Unless you live in a cave or on a deserted island, the concept of "making it on your own" is a grand myth. In the business world, it's no secret that teamwork expands mere possibilities into greater productivity and profits. My good friend Bob Kriegel, author of *If It Ain't Broke, Break It!*, *Sacred Cows Make the Best Burgers*, *Inner Skiing*, and *The C Zone*, (each book was written with someone else), became a mentor for me when in 1987 he suggested that I become a professional speaker on the subject of risk taking. Bob calls upon his expertise in peak performance as a consultant to corporations and is also a public speaker in high demand. He suggested that my adventurer's life was perhaps the path to a new career.

Although I had given hundreds of talks motivating audiences into adventure, health, and fitness, speaking to corporate audiences for a living was a new idea. Like many explorers who speak to groups, I always showed slides during my talks. In order to become a professional speaker, I needed to learn how to hold an audience with words alone, rather than hiding behind my slides as was so often the case. As my mentor, Bob became invaluable in my development as a speaker.

Partnerships are another form of teamwork. In recent years, I've grown to rely upon feedback and guidance from Sandy, who lovingly, patiently listens when I share my latest creative brainstorm.

Mentors often take the form of teachers or coaches when we're young. My very first mentor was Arthur "Pie" Meyer, my scoutmaster. Although I first joined the Boy Scouts in order to play basketball on Friday nights, he inspired me so much, I ultimately became the youngest person ever to achieve the rank of Eagle, at age twelve and a half. (Thank you, Pie. You made a major contribution to my life of adventure.)

Throughout the high points and low moments that contribute to the evidence of our lives—our accomplishments professionally, our spiritual unfolding, our blossoming as people—each of us can look back and perhaps find someone who was standing beside us as we came upon a fork in the road, confused, ill-equipped, or unable to recognize the moment as a turning point. These people, fellow travelers to be sure, may continue to show us, by their presence in our hearts, that we are never alone. At any moment we can reach back there and pull up the memory of how the help arrived and made a difference. How, when a crack appeared in our awareness, the potential breakthrough was met with precisely what was needed at exactly the moment it was called for. This helpfulness and support is something we do for each other, often without ever knowing it. Perhaps it is possible to escalate the speed and magnitude of

what seems to be a natural phenomenon of our humanness. If we can learn to open ourselves to the possibility—
even probability—that the right sort of help is always
nearby, who knows what else we may be capable of?

How to do We're a Team

Part One: Say thank-you to a mentor.

Search your past and find those people to whom you
owe a thank-you. Do what you must to track them down.
Let them know how they made a contribution to your life,
and how it made a difference. Perhaps it is discipline you
learned from your piano teacher, or measures of courage
and determination you gained from your football coach or
dance instructor. Did the drama teacher in junior high
school help you get over your shyness? What about the
person who hired you for your first job? Parents, siblings,
aunts, uncles, and grandparents are prime candidates. Another level to this exercise would be to extend it beyond
people you know and love. What about authors whose
words inspired you, or strangers whose stories were reported in the press from which you gained important insights and ideas? Make some connections between who
you are today and how the life of another person influenced you in a major way. Reflect on the myth of indepen-
dence and the truth of our interdependence.

Part Two: Create your own personal Board of Directors.

If it works in business and nonprofit organizations,
why wouldn't it be a great concept for each of us individu-
ally, too? No matter how you support yourself and your
family financially, what if you considered *your life* to be
your most important work? In this sense, the people with

whom you share your life are your investors. Almost everyone has a group of friends upon whom we call for feedback, insights, and support. Taking it to another level, perhaps we would move forward in our lives more easily if we formalized these connections and called meetings now and then to talk about big questions, changing jobs, relocating, relationship challenges, travel destinations, starting new careers, or projects we're in the middle of.

To form your Board, select at least three people whose friendship, respect, and advice you value. Invite them for a meal, provide an agenda, and listen closely to what comes up. Consider drafting a mission statement for your life, drawing up your short-term and long-range goals, and asking your Board to help keep you moving forward. This is especially valuable if you are on the verge of making gigantic changes in your life, but it works even if you are in a period of relative calm. Let your Board know that honesty is the only requirement for serving. Sometimes friends see issues in our lives more clearly than we can, but choose to spare our feelings and not volunteer what they see. Forming a team dedicated to your well-being is a powerful and rewarding way of framing your intention to stay focused in your life. The possibilities are unlimited. Spread the word, and offer to serve on someone else's personal Board in return.

In the absence of information we will fill the gaps with our biases. Don't stop once you get the "right answer." —Steven Hoffman, business consultant

Exercise 28. Sharing the Road
Monster: Contradictions

There's nothing like world travel to inspire thoughts about what it means to be a global citizen. Seeing Western material values pop up in places I'd hoped were immune is disheartening. Kayaking the mostly formerly "beautiful blue" Danube River in Hungary, we met with local environmental activists who were pessimistic about their ability to convince industrialists to take corrective measures and stop polluting the river. Near the source of the Ganges River in the foothills of the Himalayas, where modest hotels provide the bare basics for travelers and the poverty everywhere breaks your heart, the lobby's television was broadcasting the glitzy American soap opera *Santa Barbara*. In just about every third world nation you can think of, air and water pollution is common and billboards line the dusty streets. The contradictions are mind-blowing. And we have plenty of them in good old Hometown, USA, too. I think they are worth looking at for what we can learn about ourselves and our ability to accept contradictions in life as evidence of our humanness.

"Think globally, act locally" sounds right, but what does it mean, really? It is easy to be idealistic and passionate about plenty of important issues, and yet it is challenging for most of us to understand how to live, work, and play responsibly and consciously. Here are some interesting questions I puzzle over. How is it that demonstrations for peace become violent? That perhaps we help the homeless but shun our neighbors? That we make donations to aid victims of war in Bosnia, or support programs against domestic abuse, and later that day want to yell at the person who just cut us off in traffic? *And we don't see the connections.* One moment we may be placidly humming "We Are the World," and the next we're elbowing our way in line at the grocery store or the community arts and crafts festival. We may sincerely want to be enlightened, empowered by goodness, and high on life, but sometimes, frankly, it's more of a head trip. We can fool ourselves if we zone out on our own behavior in favor of passing a judgment on someone else. Maybe we need to remember that the contradictions in our lives are monsters inviting us to take another look.

Some people say that reading the newspaper guarantees a pessimistic outlook on life. Intellectually, I don't agree, but emotionally, there are days when I think they have a point. How do you keep a balanced perspective between your idealism and your realism? Whenever I've had an overdose of disturbing world headlines, I look for ways to know that my daily behavior can make a positive difference. There's so much going on that is beyond my direct control, it just makes sense to focus on making my own world a little brighter. It is good medicine. Sure we share the planet, but we also share the road.

How to do Sharing the Road

Dedicate an entire week to seeing the connections between personally enlightened and socially responsible behavior in your direct sphere of influence. Find your own little contradictions and address them. Here are more than twenty proactive examples and suggestions to get you started. Doing just one of them for a full week might be the best way to go. Start your own list and keep it going.

• Be the most courteous driver on the road. • Use your turn signals. • Drive the speed limit and • Don't tailgate. • Move to the right lane even if you are driving the legal speed, allowing faster traffic to pass easily. • Listen and observe more than you talk. • When you visit the ATM for cash and see orphaned receipts littering the ground, pick them up and put them in the trash can. • At the grocery store, push your shopping cart back in the rack where it belongs, and while you're at it, • Collect a half dozen other stray carts, too. • And if you have more then ten items, don't stand in the Express Lane. • Return your library books on time. • Give people flowers for no reason. • Pay your traffic tickets. • Pay the bridge, road, or parking toll for the person behind you. • Straighten the magazines in your dentist's waiting room. • Use the pooper scooper when you walk your dog. • Turn down the stereo. • Clean out your closets and donate things you aren't using to the Salvation Army or Goodwill. • Don't talk at the movie theater. • Wait your turn, or better yet, • Let someone go in front of you. • Pass out compliments like confetti.

> *Let there be peace on earth, and let it begin with me.*
> —Sy Miller and Jill Jackson

Exercise 29. Climb Your Family Tree
Monster: The Past

When **Alex Haley wrote** *Roots,* he presented the world with a colossal gift. *Roots* spoke deeply and passionately to the importance of knowing who and where we come from in order to more fully know who we are. To own the greater past of our ancestors for better or worse casts a spotlight on the unseen influences on our personalities and our character. We can more fully understand why we are the way we are by doing a little research into our family tree.

In my own case, the deck was stacked for me to become an adventurer. My grandfather, born in 1838, traveled across America in a covered wagon with his wife and five children. Thirty years later, a widower, he remarried. He was sixty-five years old, living three blocks from Monterey's Cannery Row, when my father was born. My dad went to Stanford with John Steinbeck in the early 1920s and learned marine biology working with Doc Rickets, the inspiration for Steinbeck's main character in the novel *Cannery Row*. Dad worked his way through Stanford Medical School. One of his projects involved doing biological research in Alaska. While tagging salmon, he shot and killed the largest Kodiak bear ever recorded. From this bloodline I also have a half-uncle who sailed clipper ships around Cape Horn.

My mother, born in Princeton, New Jersey, lived according to her heart, unafraid of the opinions of others. As a young, bright single woman she turned her secretarial skills into a career and eventually became the executive secretary to the president of AT&T in New York. She married her girlfriend's father. He was a doctor who, soon after their marriage, served in the military in the South Pacific. They lived in Manila. General Douglas MacArthur and his wife and General and Madame Chiang Kai-shek were among her friends. After divorcing her husband—a bold thing to do in those days—she met my father in Shanghai. Thanks to her bloodline I am related to A.A. Milne, from whom I got my middle name and a genetic connection to Christopher Robin and Pooh Bear.

I was once asked, "Of all the interesting people you've met in your life, who is the *most* interesting?" I did a quick mental scan of all the highly visible celebrities and the most extraordinary humans I'd shared a little time with. It didn't take long to come up with the right answer. "My mother and father," I said.

Maybe you'll find writers, explorers, artists, and inventors in your family tree. Or politicians, social reformers, and teachers. Or colorful scalawags, pirates, and gangsters. Maybe there's an entire bloodline you never knew existed due to secret liaisons in your distant, distant past that have never been openly shared.

Who knows what sort of curious, vital, or liberating information is back there waiting to be discovered? Perhaps you'll find evidence to help explain certain passions or interests you've maintained since you were young, but could never satisfactorily explain. If you wonder why you favor cold weather over warm, love certain kinds of music but not others, have a talent for writing, or a hot temper that puzzles you, perhaps the answers will be found in your genes. Instead of going through life as disconnected from your heritage as an unsolved mystery, why not explore it? For added motivation, think about it as a favor to your children. Pass it on.

How to do Climb Your Family Tree

Part One: Immediate family.

Spend time interviewing every living relative, beginning with your parents if possible, realizing that a time may come when you no longer have the opportunity. If people are scattered across the country and throughout the world, this will require quite a bit of time, so set your pace accordingly. Ask them simple questions about their lives as kids. Probe their memories of Christmas celebrations, family dinnertime, a typical Sunday, school lessons and teachers. Who were their friends, mentors, and enemies? Find the major influences in their lives. Try to get a clear picture of what it was like to be them before you came along. Make it easier with tape recorders, as well as still and video cameras for capturing antiques and old photos. Build your files of information for the purpose of sharing it with your own children some day.

Part Two: Visit your roots.

Investigate your family tree beyond your grandparents, going as far back as the research will take you. Once you are satisfied the job is complete, plan one or more trips to visit the most significant places in your story, especially those with which you feel a special connection. If those places happen to be on foreign soil, so much the better. Purposeful travel is the very best kind.

> *"When you wake up in the morning, Pooh," said Piglet at last, "what's the first thing you say to yourself?"*
> *"What's for breakfast?" said Pooh. "What do you say, Piglet?"*
> *"I say, I wonder what's going to happen exciting today?" said Piglet.*
> *Pooh nodded thoughtfully.*
> *It's the same thing," he said.*
> —A.A. Milne, *Winnie-the-Pooh*

Exercise 30. The Mouse That Roared
Monster: Self-Confidence

I **first became affiliated** with Earth House, a residential
alternative treatment center for kids with major mental disorders near Princeton, New Jersey, in 1973 when Rosalind
LaRoche, its founder, contacted me after hearing about my
work with ex-convicts and recovering drug addicts. Each
Friday that I wasn't somewhere else in the world, I went
to Earth House to lead classes in the yoga-based exercise
program I had designed for the patients. It is the nature of
schizophrenia to be so intensely debilitating that those who
suffer from it are very disconnected from their bodies. Exercise, while mostly unappealing to schizophrenics, was
producing very positive side effects in addition to promot-
ing more health in their bodies. Encouraged by the results
we were seeing, I wanted to push the concept a little more.
But my only credentials were personal experiences, and I
wasn't sure I should speak up about an idea that had been
brewing privately for some weeks. . . .

Heading into a staff meeting one day, I decided to share
my idea. But once the meeting was underway, the words
stuck in my throat. Would they laugh me out of the room?
Was the idea totally outrageous? To my knowledge, there
was no evidence, no experiments or precedents to refer to.
It was unparalleled. Finally, in spite of myself, I found the
courage. I stated that I wanted to take the patients on a
wilderness adventure. I explained that personally, I had received so much benefit from the challenge of outdoor adventure, I wondered if the rewards would translate for the
patients as well.

Everyone at the meeting literally laughed out loud at the
idea . . . except Rosalind. Over fifty "Earth Adventures" and

many years later, we can look back at some marvelous successes. I'm so glad the idea didn't stay stuck in my throat.

In the real spirit of *Hug the Monster*, we can all use more practice at being the authority in our own lives, and stepping out there on a limb now and then. Not having certain scholarly credentials may prevent you from getting a job teaching in a university or being interviewed by the press as an expert, but why should it stop you from speaking up in a meeting and sharing what may just be the breakthrough idea that's needed to solve a problem? Perhaps this has happened to you: You sit there in a meeting wondering if you should speak up, and ten minutes later, someone else across the table expresses a similar idea and it is met with great enthusiasm. The accolades, satisfaction—even promotion—could have been yours.

How to do The Mouse That Roared

Are you timid and shy? Afraid of being embarrassed or flatly rejected by your peers? Or, do you often avoid speaking up so that you won't inherit the responsibility that might come along with the suggestion you are secretly eager to make? Have you ever considered the possibility that you hold 50 percent of the solution, and that speaking up will evoke a response in someone else at the table that leads to an even better idea? Some of the best ideas and greatest accomplishments are wrapped up in the spirit of teamwork.

Try to keep this in mind: *You are not your idea.* If the idea is rejected, it doesn't mean that you will also be rejected as a person, right? Consider couching your idea in the context of brainstorming. Or put the shoe on the other foot: How do you react when someone else speaks up? Being supportive of others will make it easier when it is your turn to take a similar risk. Experiment a little bit. Doing this exercise doesn't mean you have to totally transform your personality. Focus on the outcome and all of the ways in which your idea may produce unimagined benefits for everyone involved. Review the five-step method for How to Hug a Monster and let it work for you. Before announcing your idea at the real meeting, practice by trying your idea out first in private with your spouse, partner, or a good friend. Rehearse in front of the mirror, or into a tape recorder. Make notes and take them with you to the meeting. To do this exercise and hug the monster, you have to stand up for your ideas in a meeting. Whatever the outcome is, you will automatically win, and so will everyone else.

> *The greatest talent is the ability to strip a theory*
> *until the simple basic idea emerges with clarity.*
> —Albert Einstein

Exercise 31. POV
Monster: Diversity

In screenwriting and filmmaking, POV is shorthand for *point of view*. It is a reference to whose eyes the camera will be "seeing" through. Remember the film *Jaws*? In the opening scenes, the camera gave us the experience of swimming in the ocean, unaware that a killer shark was nearby. Later, we felt we were on the platform of the boat along with Richard Dreyfuss, Roy Scheider, and Robert Shaw waiting for the killer shark to surface. Character POV adds intensity and helps the audience step into the character's shoes. As a metaphor, POV reminds us we can do the same in order to understand a little more clearly what it might be like to "be" another person. It is especially useful for hugging the monsters that separate us from people who are different from us. Prejudice and cultural isolation generally go hand in hand with fear and ignorance. I've encountered it again and again in my adventures around the world, as well as at home. Here are a few especially memorable encounters with POV.

When Cherif, a Tunisian, and I were planning our kayak journey on the Nile River, one of the issues was food. Another was the possibility of theft. Because Cherif spoke Arabic, we decided I would stay behind and guard our kayaks and gear while he ventured into the villages for our supplies. The joke was on us as we soon realized that the Nubians who live between Khartoum and Egypt have a reputation for being extremely honest. The fear of being ripped off was totally misplaced.

The scene was intense stepping out of the taxi at the port in Port-au-Prince, Haiti. Donkey carts filled with local produce crowded the streets. Laborers heaved and hoisted cargo boxes. Human cranes lifted pallets and rolled oil drums from here to there, their muscles glistening in the midday sun. Everywhere the combination of heat, sweat, and dust made the atmosphere heavy and thick. My own thoughts were difficult to hear above the yelling, arguing, and laughter that filled the air. I was so captured by what I was taking in that I was slow to realize my camera bag and other gear were still in the backseat of the cab, and the windows were down. The driver, seeing my concern, shouted, "No problem. It is safe here in Haiti." I shot him a look as if to say, "Sure, pal. Do you think I just got off the boat?" But he was right. I eventually made three different trips to Haiti and never once had a bad experience.

Driving with friends near the Taos Pueblo, I was interested in going on a run when I spotted a man who was jogging, so I hopped out of the vehicle and caught up to him. His name was Benny. We ran together for two hours, and afterward he invited me to his home for dinner and to meet his parents. Hanging on the wall of his humble adobe house was a photograph of his father shaking hands with President Nixon in the Oval Office. To my complete surprise, I was in the home of a very wise and important man—the chief of the Taos Pueblo Indians who had recently secured the return of forty-eight thousand acres of sacred land to his people. Later, Benny bestowed a huge honor on me when he invited me to climb the sacred mountain of the Pueblo with him, a place where "white man" was not allowed to go.

For a period of several years, my son, Daren, always wore baggy pants, an extra-large white T-shirt, and a shaved head. It was the uniform look of his self-selected peer group known to the rest of us as "skaters." In groups of four or five, skateboards always in tow, they spent endless hours together, practicing and performing their tricks anywhere they could find concrete, curbs, raised obstacles, or smooth asphalt parking lots. From the point of view of most adults, especially owners of the lots on which they skated, they were a menace, not to mention a potential legal liability as they jumped obstacles, defying gravity with their tricks. And they *looked* so messy. As Daren's father, I longed to see him dressed in clothes his own size— a nice pair of slacks and a polo shirt, for example, a manner of dress that guaranteed total humiliation for him. But as an athlete myself, I was in awe of the way he and his friends could perform a jump and manage to keep the board stuck to their feet without glue. These guys are athletic rebels who represent a new wave—surfers without water. Whether they like it or not, they are fantastic athletes.

I realize I am fortunate, that it isn't possible for everyone to be as exposed to life around the planet as I have been. Adventure travel as a crosscultural tool is one way to unlearn the spiritual violence of prejudice and to celebrate human diversity. The tapestry of my own life is woven from the threads of the people of many nations. Yet here in the States, my work has exposed me to a host of subcultures as well—from prisoners, mental patients, and hippies to CEOs, Hollywood superstars, and pro football players. My own POV is constantly stretched, challenged, and enriched. Continual exposure, interaction, and friendships with all kinds of people is a fantastic way to live a full and interesting life. I can't imagine living any other way. And I want this way of living to be the thing my kids inherit from me; passing it on to them and they in turn to their children is perhaps the most meaningful work of the collective human family.

How to do POV

Part One: In your immediate world.

In building relationships, it is second nature to look for things we have in common with others. We tend to connect through similarities. But what about the differences? As an exercise in observation, take a closer look at the people in your own world—neighbors, coworkers, friends, employees at stores and other businesses you frequent. *What is it like to be them?* Paying attention to skin color, speech patterns, body types, sexual orientation, cultural expressions, habits, phobias, upbringing, religious affiliations, economic realities, talents, and personality traits will get you started. Instead of seeing how they are like you, see how they are unlike you. Perhaps you'll gain new levels of appreciation for diversity by having conversations that speak to their own unique qualities. Go people-watching in a public place and be like a camera with a POV other than your own. Or establish your POV objectively, as if you were watching exquisite birds or beautiful animals at the zoo.

Once you've made a practice of connecting via the differences you've discovered, with more facts and insights at your disposal, your relationships may be better balanced, more authentic, and less likely to be filled with your own projections. Instead of taking life so personally, you can relax and enjoy whatever comes your way, regardless of how similar or different it is from you.

Part Two: Multicultural adventures.

Make a commitment to learning about cultures other than your own. Here are some ideas to get you started planning a full year of multicultural adventures.

Whatever your strong interest is—music, art, theater, crafts, religion, sports, health and healing, literature—take up a multicultural view for a while. Attend concerts of Indian music or Japanese art. Participate in Mexican-American, African-American, and Native American festivals. Explore the diverse religions in your community by attending worship services—imagine you are Buddhist, Catholic, Hindu, Jewish, Unitarian, Greek Orthodox, Presbyterian, Muslim, or Pentecostal for a day, to name only a few. Expose yourself to alternative methods of health and healing—have an acupuncture session, or visit a Chinese herbalist. Dedicate one day a week to eating foreign food and ethnic cuisine until you've exhausted the possibilities in your city. Get involved in your local school's exchange-student program. Take advantage of programs offered by the public library. If you are in business, make connections with those in your community who are involved in importing and exporting. Sign up for language classes at your local community college. Instead of a traditional Christmas, this year find out how your ancestors celebrated the holiday, or how your neighbors from Brazil, Manila, Kenya, and Mexico do it, and make it a global celebration. Use your imagination and you'll discover new exciting worlds in your own hometown.

Part Three: Says who?

The word *disability* may be necessary for insurance companies and lawyers, but ask anyone who lives with the classification and you may discover a real treasure. The athletes who compete in the Special Olympics come to mind. We sometimes pass premature judgment on others because we see clothing, circumstances, and/or life experiences we'd rather not have ourselves. What makes you turn your head and look the other way? Physical realities such as old age, wheelchairs, or a seeing-eye dog leading someone across the street? Maybe it is people who openly, freely express their identities with tattoos, long hair, and leather. Or white middle-class yuppies. Perhaps it is same-sex couples holding hands. Or the shaven heads and saffron robes of devotees. Or homeless beggars pushing shopping carts filled with other people's discards. Find out what your hot buttons are, where your prejudice hasn't yet been challenged, and take some action to educate yourself. The goal is eliminating judgments that are based on lack of experience and ignorance.

"Namaste"
— greeting in India.
Translation: *"I honor the light within you."*

Chapter Six

The Freedom Monsters

Exercise	Monster
32. The Looking Glass	**Self-Image**
33. Blind Walk	**Trust**
34. Face the Lion	**Anxiety and Low Energy**
35. Give a Speech	**Being Judged**
36. Handle a Snake	**No Daring**
37. Go on a Vision Quest	**Transformation**
38. Find Your LifeSport	**Vitality and Longevity**
39. Passages	**No Growth**
40. Never Give Up	**Justifying Barriers**
41. Masai Stand	**Staying Grounded**
42. White-water Rafting	**Outrageous Fun**
43. Do You Wanna Dance?	**Nothing to Celebrate**

To act with the spirit of adventure is to dive *heart first* into the present moment where, again and again, we discover that we are always free. To suspend certain memories—data about who and where we have been in the past—and participate in adventure is an invitation to connect with our essential selves. In this way, Freedom Monsters are the fearful responses that can block us from being in that place inside where love, joy, compassion, and a state of flow are our natural resources. Freedom Monsters can cause us to cling to the past, cluttering the landscape with conditions and facts. They argue for our limitations because they are charged with maintaining our security, however we define it.

Freedom Monsters have two useful personalities, and you don't get to fully appreciate both sides—the mundane and the magical—unless you get to know them. Until they are hugged, Freedom Monsters most often act as the law enforcement officers of our inner lives. They patrol the uncelebrated, unconstrained borders between two territories—the known and the unknown. They shout, "Halt, who goes there?" whenever we challenge the status quo. In this capacity, their job is to protect and defend our identity, remind us of the rules, and keep us safe traveling on the well-worn straight-and-narrow path. But beware. In this mode, so security-conscious are the Freedom Monsters that they've perfected intricate schemes and brilliant strategies for preventing the new, the untried, unexpressed, and never-before-felt experiences of life.

To take the metaphor a few steps further, they sometimes collaborate with the Logic Monsters to enforce the rules; with the Inertia Monsters when a breakthrough to action is about to happen; and the Relationship Monsters when strong feelings of all kinds—from paralyzing fear to total compassion—threaten to overwhelm us. When a Freedom Monster teams up with another monster, it's as if they all increase exponentially.

"I could never do that" is the statement we make when Freedom Monsters catch us hesitating at the border, still in known territory. "Yes I can!" is what you declare as you hug them and cross into unknown territory. Although they can show up any time and under any circumstance, here are a few examples of Freedom Monster breakthrough moments: You go backpacking for a week in the woods instead of doing the more familiar and comfortable *tennis-resort-at-the-beach-in-a-nice-hotel* kind of vacation; you drop the "dress for success" attire of classic suits and pumps in favor of lively colors, softer lines, and individual expression; you downsize your life, resign from your job as director of human resources, live off your savings account, and do something else for a year like travel, volunteer for a charitable cause, write a novel, or get certified in a skill like scuba diving or a trade such as massage therapy. Experiment with your identity, your talents, and your wish list, and you are bound to meet the Freedom Monsters.

When you hug a Freedom Monster and go for the unknown, the "yes!" energy can be like an atomic blast in the solar plexus, triggering a predictable cycle of sensations. First we feel anxious. Tension mounts, giving way to concentration and exhilaration for the task which, when completed, transforms into euphoria. Finally, we feel a wonderful release. Simultaneous with the hug, we flush with pulse-quickening excitement and feel our entire being expand to new possibilities. The thrill of being alive is unmistakable. In addition to the energy rush in the moment of the hug, the effects tend to be wider, deeper, and longer lasting. New possibilities sprout and options expand. Many-layered and multifaceted, hugging a Freedom Monster offers you direct access to your Source, and in the process produces the kind of confidence, courage, and compassion that can bring about wholesale change in our lives. There's a great line in the movie *Green Card* when Andie McDowell's character says of Gerard Depardieu's character in describing his irrepressible, insatiable zest for living, "He *eats* life." That's how it is with the Freedom Monsters. They are all about movement, creativity, connection, and celebration in the moment they are hugged.

Regardless of which territory you are in when you meet up with one, the energetic Freedom Monsters remind us that life is filled with surprises. If you pretend that life is 100 percent controllable from a set of rules, perhaps you are anesthetized from life's pain, but it works both ways— you may not get to feel your own joy, either. By accident or on purpose, Freedom Monsters are destined to be hugged; in other words, *they are our response to circumstances* that threaten to shake things up, send us on an adventure we didn't plan to have, and test both the quality and degree of trust we can place in ourselves, others, and the environment. In ancient Eastern spiritual terms, it could be called "trusting the Tao"—the natural order of things.

The good news is that when you hug Freedom Monsters you are on *their turf* in the unknown territory where they quite often demonstrate stupendous, even miraculous talents once they've been unleashed. Dedicated not only to your security but *to your total well-being*, the Freedom Monsters are resourceful beyond logic and loving beyond limits, giving you access to parts of yourself you may not have known existed and inviting other parts to finally bloom for the first time. While the other monsters may stand clearly between you and your fears, the Freedom Monsters navigate the distance between you, your fears, *and your dreams.*

Exercise 32. The Looking Glass
Monster: Self-Image

Living and working in foreign countries, I've always made a practice of dressing in native garb, and over the years I've rarely hesitated to experiment with a variety of clothing and hair styles, from Levi's and T-shirts to Italian-made suits and ties, from shoulder-length hair in a ponytail to short, razor cut styles and everything in between. I suppose we all make a certain number of concessions to comfort in order to maintain the look and style called for in our jobs. Who wouldn't rather be wearing comfortable sweats most of the time if we could? During the 1980s the trend was power suits for power lunches. The '90s have introduced a more relaxed dress code into corporate and business settings, along with brown bag lunches in the park followed by a power *walk*. The result, some say, is increased productivity, job satisfaction, and creativity. The way we look affects the way we feel. *We know this.* Yet no matter what the fashion trends dictate, we are attached to our appearance in ways that can throw personal growth into a holding pattern.

The mirror is a monster for a lot of people. So are vanity, fashion, and peer pressure. An image consultant once told me it is fairly common for clients to insist they want help changing the way they look, only to let their new, expensive wardrobes hang in the closet for months, unable to embrace the new image they've invested in. Thanks to medical science and technology, along with being better informed about such things as health, nutrition, and exercise, we as a culture are pushing back the traditional markers of middle age and old age. But can we enjoy living and looking younger while remembering that every stage of life has plenty to celebrate, especially our hard-earned maturity?

As a Freedom Monster, acquiring and maintaining the "right look" can also become a time-consuming, budget-draining hobby if we begin to believe that the outside is more important than the inside. We can use appearance to make a statement, fit in with our peer group, or bolster self-esteem just as easily as it can hide certain insecurities and even prevent us from ever doing anything about them. How secure are you when it comes to the way you look?

How to do the Looking Glass

Part One: Stand in front of the mirror.

Ask yourself these questions. What parts of your appearance are you attached to the most? What are your best features? Which ones do you wish were different? What do you complain about? Is there something about the way you look that keeps you from total self-acceptance? Do you wish you were thinner, fatter, taller, shorter? That your hair was longer, shorter, curlier, straighter, lighter, darker? That your breasts were fuller? Chest broader? Waist trimmer? Thighs slimmer? What features or styles cause envy about the way other people look? Do you draw your ideals from movie stars, professional athletes, and fashion models? Where does your self-image come from? As a kid, were you teased about a funny-shaped nose, big ears, or crooked teeth? Discover everything you love and hate about the way you look. Don't hold back. Finally, what can you control and/or change, and what must you simply accept? In both cases, begin to take the action called for. As your daily meditation for one week, love yourself unconditionally.

Part Two: Play image consultant.

Have you ever found yourself thinking, "Gee, he'd be nicer looking if only . . ." or, "She would be so pretty if she would just . . ."? If so, chances are someone has thought the same thing about you! For fun, get a second opinion from someone you love and respect. Would a new style of dressing be more flattering? How about your current hairstyle or color? What are you willing to change about the way you look in response to some honest feedback? Be brave. Ask. For balance, invite your volunteer image consultant to play a round of "Do You Know What I Like about You?" at the end of your session.

Part Three: Change your appearance.

Change your style. Be bold. Cut your hair. Become a red-head. Wear delicate patterns and soft colors if you always wear bold solids. Put on heels and a miniskirt if you always appear in long skirts and flats. Exchange conservative ties for whimsical ones, casual sweaters for suit coats, and colored shirts for the white ones. Wear a T-shirt under your best suit, or sneakers with a fancy dress. If you rarely wear cosmetics, use eyeliner, mascara, and lipstick. Get a dramatic makeover. Be a hippie for a day. Or a fashion plate. If you normally dress down, dress up. If you normally dress up, wear sweats. Break your patterns and see how it feels inside when you look different on the outside.

> *The true value of a human being is determined*
> *primarily by the measure and sense in which he has*
> *attained liberation from the self.* —Albert Einstein

Exercise 33. Blind Walk
Monster: Trust

The exotic sounds and spicy and putrid scents of the Casbah in Tangier came alive for me when I performed an event I named the Blind Walk as part of my Everyman's Olympics, an Adventure Decathlon. The object was to take away my eyesight and successfully navigate through the maze of shops and stalls, turning a "handicap" into an asset. I used double blindfolds made of cotton and black patches so that no light could come through. The walk was two miles from start to finish through streets so narrow and confusing that tourists with their eyes wide open almost always get lost. My broom-handle walking stick became my eyes, and children helped direct me, especially with their giggling and laughing. All of my senses intensified, and to my amazement I experienced a flow state normally associated with peak performance in athletics. Surprisingly, I never felt embarrassment even when I heard laughter because I couldn't see any faces.

I am inspired when I listen to blind or deaf people talk about how richly they experience the world, especially those who've never seen a sunrise or the face of their beloved, or heard a Chopin piano concerto or the gentle cooing of a newborn baby. It is difficult not to feel sorry for them, but I know better. If blind people see in ways sighted people cannot, then we must conclude that nature adjusts her gifts for each of us. Apparently we all have a much greater capacity to use our inner senses than we know.

When leading team-building exercises and games, I often use some variation of the Blind Walk where participants must hold one another's hands and navigate an obstacle course through trust and a heightened awareness of one another.

When we alter our senses, we get to experience our bodies in new and different ways. Often, as was the case for me in the Casbah, in doing so we'll discover a state of being that is like flowing, an effortless and fully alive sensation that suggests new possibilities for daily *sighted* living, too.

How to do Blind Walk

Select your route in advance. You can rehearse it with eyes open, or simply practice "being blind" around the house, or walking from your office to the water cooler with your eyes shut. Ask a friend to accompany you on the day of your Blind Walk. Make sure it is a distance that will challenge you. Cover your eyes with a dark scarf or patches. Make sure no light at all comes through. Then, simply pay attention by using your other senses. Use a walking stick. If you are feeling really adventurous, take the bus to a pre-determined destination where a friend will meet you. The power in this exercise is in the *doing*, and not simply imagining what it would be like.

> *The best moments usually occur when a person's body*
> *or mind is stretched to its limits in a voluntary effort*
> *to accomplish something difficult and worthwhile.*
> —Mihaly Csikszentmihalyi

Exercise 34. Face the Lion
Monster: Anxiety and Low Energy

I have learned to think of stress as extra energy begging to be spent. The real trick in managing stress is knowing how to recognize and use the release valve. A brisk walk or jog. Deep breathing. Stretching. Worry beads. Less caffeine. Soft music. A closed door. Everyone has tips on how to handle stress. We also know the ideal way to stay healthy is to balance the effects with adequate sleep, regular exercise, a nutritious diet, and time off to unwind. Realistically, however, it's also a good idea to have a few tricks up your sleeve. Here are two exercises, The Lion Hunt Jump, and the Lion Roar, that work wonders when the adrenaline has been flowing overtime and we have miles to go before we can rest.

I learned the Lion Hunt Jump from the Masai and Samburu warriors in Kenya. It's a ritual dance intended to transform adrenaline into courage. It also guarantees that you are in your body instead of only in your head with the fear. Doing it right guarantees a surge of confidence that lasts long enough to be successful in whatever you're about to do. When it's a jungle out there and hunting lions is on your to do list, a few minutes of jumping and grunting like a Masai warrior will chase away the jitters and get you moving.

The Lion Roar is my own version of a hatha yoga posture known as the Lion. I once led a yoga session for six Danish models who were working on location in the exotic gardens of Marrakech, Morocco. As you'll find out for yourself in a moment, doing this exercise requires stretching, scrunching, and contorting your face. In the class, when we got to the Lion pose one of the models just couldn't make herself do it. Her monster was vanity and she couldn't bring herself to hug it. She shook her head "no" and adamantly refused to make herself ugly, even for a moment.

Corporate audiences are more adventurous. When I give presentations I always demonstrate both the Lion Hunt Jump and the Lion Roar and ask everyone to participate. Even though doing them can be embarrassing in a crowd of one's peers, I love how playful people become. It melts the ice and warms up the room faster than just about anything else I know.

How to do the Lion Hunt Jump

How do you prepare yourself to do something scary? Here's a fun method of charging your nervous system with bravery. Fear produces adrenaline that's intended for immediate use in a fight-or-flight response. Having a success ritual can be worth a million bucks, and make you feel that

way, too. When you start to feel butterflies in your stomach, do this exercise to chase them away. If you don't redi-
rect your adrenaline, you run a greater risk of overwork-
ing your nervous system. The result can be anything from
a sick feeling that dampens your senses to a flash of anger
at an innocent coworker or family member. Cool out—
jump like a brave hunter instead. The energy that we associate with fear can work to our advantage.

This is a ritual exercise. You are going to learn to jump
up and land on your feet a new way. Typically we land on
our toes and balls of the feet when we jump up and down,
squat, or jump rope. In jumping exercises of all kinds,
rarely does the heel touch the ground. This exercise will deliver a different sensation—a bit of a shock on the soles of
your feet. Although breaking the pattern of more familiar
jumping is not necessarily the point, you will have to override instincts and former learning to do it correctly. Unless
you stay aware of the exact directions you will not land on
your heels. The effects are pretty profound when done
properly.

Stand erect with your feet as far apart as the width of
your shoulders. With your arms hanging relaxed at your
sides, jump an inch off the ground and land on the entire
length of your feet. If you do it right, you'll give your entire
body a nice grounding jolt. Each time you land, bring up a
deep, loud "grunt" or "who" from your belly. The deeper
the better. Continue to jump higher until you've reached
your vertical jump limit. Get psyched up!

In addition to grunting, the lion-hunting warriors of East
Africa also chant about all of the lions they have killed.
Whether their stories are fact or fiction doesn't seem to
matter. The intention of the exercise is to get themselves
revved up. Use this silly-looking but powerful technique

as preparation for successfully meeting a challenge. As you do the Lion Hunt Jump, be completely in your body, feel all *of your feelings*, and picture your success. Before a big presentation or confrontation, do this a few times in your office and ignore your snickering colleagues . . . you're about to score a big one. Use it any time you want or need to energize yourself fast.

How to do the Lion Roar

In yoga, the posture begins in a relaxed position, sitting either on the ground with legs crossed or in a chair. Rest your hands on your knees. Inhale deeply through your nostrils. Slowly, deliberately release the breath as you open your throat with a deep guttural "roar" and stick your tongue out, trying to touch your chin with it. At the same time, roll your eyes back as far as they can go, as if looking over your head, and stretch your fingers apart. Be sure to keep your throat open as you roar. A closed throat can irritate your vocal chords.

Some people call this an instant face-lift because it removes tension from facial muscles, eases eye strain, and stimulates circulation. Do it several times a day to feel more relaxed and look like an alert, contented cat. What the Lion Hunt Jump does for the neck down, this one does for the neck up. It puts a smile on your face.

> *Great ideas originate in the muscles.*
> —Thomas Edison

Exercise 35. Give a Speech
Monster: Being Judged

Stop **right there.** Don't skip this one, please. It's too valu-able and way too easy to do, once you learn the trick. Here it is, based on my experience. I became an adventurer by swimming the Golden Gate. I swam the Gate by getting in shape, and I got in shape by first knowing that I wasn't in shape . . . so, it began with getting in the pool and swimming two laps. There was no way I could have done it *by pretending that I was in shape.*

I remember my very first speech. I was thirteen, and had been invited to emcee the annual meeting of my Boy Scout troop. A supposed honor, I was given the job because I had achieved the level of Eagle Scout six months earlier. I was the youngest Eagle Scout in the world, so I guess my scout-master thought I could do anything. But I was scared out of my wits about getting up to speak in front of one hundred other Boy Scouts and their parents. I went to the circus that afternoon to take my mind off of it. Looking for a good ex-cuse to back out, I made myself sick—a combination of nerves and overeating—and phoned the scoutmaster to an-nounce I was ill and unable to do the job. Rather than ac-cepting my story, he drove over to my house and dragged me to the meeting, where, to my surprise, I did just great. Thank goodness he didn't let me take the coward's way out. Four decades and hundreds of speeches later, in retro-spect it was a defining moment in my development.

Public speaking is about setting a goal, gathering infor-mation, developing it, practicing it, setting the date, and stor-ing up endurance to use in the performance. I'm a far better speaker now than I was in the beginning. It isn't about being clever or having nerves of steel at all. It's about practice.

How to Give a Speech

According to some pollsters, giving a talk in public is our number one fear in life. We are more afraid of giving a speech than we are of death, snakes, and spiders. Risking public humiliation is a hero's adventure for sure, since that's how most people feel about giving a talk in front of an audience. It's rarely humiliating and often the best ego booster imaginable. Your best strategy for maintaining resolve has to do with picking a topic that will hold your own attention. What do you know a lot about? If you don't have an area of expertise, what topic do you want to learn more about? The bottom line here is that you are going to give a speech. Will you speak to a group of friends, strangers, a church group or service club? How about the PTA? Is there a new policy coming up for review at the next school board meeting that you feel strongly about?

Set the date, then rehearse. Know your audience and prepare accordingly. Go to a park and practice giving your speech to the trees, birds, and blue sky. Practice into a tape recorder and/or stand in front of a mirror. Or have a conversation with a friend in which you inject your key points. Will you work from notes? It's completely up to you, of course, but the high might be even higher afterward if you don't use notes. *Secret: Your confidence as well as your skill will come from your preparation.* Do the butterflies ever go away completely before a speech? Actually, they do, but it takes a lot of experience to get to that point. Until they do, I can assure you that *they aren't fatal.* Hugging this monster is a liberating experience.

> *Over the piano was printed a notice: Please do not shoot the pianist. He is doing his best.* —Oscar Wilde

Exercise 36. Handle a Snake
Monster: No Daring

When people hear about my adventures in the bush, a frequent question is "What about the snakes?" Over the years, my answer has developed several levels to it. I admit that learning to handle a snake hasn't come easily, and I've had some practice. Of all the world's snakes, only a few are actually aggressive. Among those are the cobra and its cousin, the mamba. Both inhabit the places in which I have spent time. Before a solo trek over the High Atlas Mountains and the Sahara Desert, my research included learning about the pit viper, a snake attracted by heat and common to the area I would be trekking. One writer's encounter with pit vipers included the story of a moonlit night during which he counted twenty of them in, under, and around his tent. Although I promptly exchanged my brand-new tent for a better, more secure, snake-proof one, I didn't see a single pit viper on the trek. One morning in Kenya, we heard rustling in the foot-high grass. I quickly shot a glance in the direction of the sound and saw the black tail of a snake. From twenty feet away, Lambat, my guide, raised his arm, hand cupped slightly to pantomime the message "cobra!" The snakes were definitely out there, but like so many of the animals, this one was moving out of our way.

I held a cobra once in Morocco. I've been close to cobras in India and watched with fascination as handlers demonstrated how venom is extracted and used for medicine. They are a chilling sight to see, especially with their awesome hoods flared and fangs exposed. Yet the handlers were informed, skilled, and experienced enough to walk among dozens of them at a time, casually moving out of the way of striking cobras.

My most meaningful experience with a snake wasn't in the bush at all, but rather, at the Randall Junior Museum in San Francisco, where the snake handler draped a ten-foot-long python around my shoulders like a shawl. I felt a warm sense of awe and respect as the beefy snake, six inches in diameter, constricted its muscles around me . . . and a sense of real connection with it once we were face to face, eyeball to eyeball, its curious tongue pointing directly at me. Its movements felt more like communication than a threat; perhaps it was even offering me a hug. The intelligence and awareness the python conveyed were a kind of awakening for me. It was the first time I understood how people have snakes as pets.

For many people, the mere mention of the word snake or the mental exercise "imagine a snake in the room with you" can trigger a good case of the heebie-jeebies. But, contrary to common belief, snakes are mostly harmless, non-poisonous, and unless they've just slithered out of water, are not even slimy. They are dry to the touch. Instinctive fear of all snakes might be our genetic inheritance. If you have such a fear, the question is, how can that fear serve you? What's the payoff if you hug it? Want to find out?

How to do Handle a Snake

Although I continue to get over my fear of snakes, I no longer have a phobia because I have been exposed to many kinds and under lots of different circumstances. For example, I know that once I have my hand on the back of the snake's head, I'm okay. Because I've learned to do it, so can you. How does this translate into a better life? Simple. It's just about getting over another fear. If you prove to yourself that you can handle a snake, what else might that prove in the process?

Visit your local zoo, a science museum, or an alligator/reptile farm where the public is invited to experience snakes firsthand, supervised by trained handlers. Handle a snake. Take your camera and make sure someone captures the moment on film.

This exercise may be just the antivenom your spirit needs to heal the sting of boredom and/or mediocrity that has slithered into your life undetected. If you want to get charged up about making other changes in your life, go handle a snake and hug a monster.

> *You get to the point where your demons, which are terrifying, get smaller and smaller, and you get bigger and bigger.*   —August Wilson

Exercise 37. Go on a Vision Quest
Monster: Transformation

The day was filled with unmistakable irony when the seeds for my own vision quest were planted. I was in Morocco training to swim from Africa to Europe, but another piece of business was nearby. Two months earlier I had been cast to do a television commercial as the guy who would "walk a mile for a Camel." The original script called for filming the commercial in Egypt, with me walking through the desert and around the pyramids. But when the political climate became too hot, the location was changed to Marrakech, Morocco. The memory is especially sharp because I met the film crew in Casablanca on the first day of the Arab-Israeli Six Day War.

In the camel market outside Marrakech, I was both a

participant and an observer. The exacting work of the American film crew only magnified the feelings that had begun to well up inside me, their businesslike precision playing counterpoint to the chaotic, intense scene in the loud, dusty market where Arabs and Berbers, sweating in their rancid wool robes, plied their trade. The ready-made scene had a natural sound track, too—an odd symphony of brass bells, the flat alto braying of donkeys, and camels coughing and barking like baritone drunks. In the one hundred–degree heat, I listened to the director explain the sequence of shots while the makeup artist tried to keep my makeup fresh with more powder to soak up the perspiration. But my thoughts were totally absorbed in a more striking, interior scene.

I was thinking about *Siddhartha,* the Hermann Hesse story about a young man who rejects his comfortable life in search of greater meaning and purpose. My studies in comparative religion and various spiritual/metaphysical teachings were beginning to take hold as I saw myself that day. I took an inventory. The clothes I wore were not mine. My hair was freshly cut and styled for the film image. I wondered, *What is there of me in here?* Even my thoughts were not my own. *What did I know?* The connections I had begun to make through my athletic adventures were demanding more of me.

Fifty miles in the distance loomed the snow-capped High Atlas Mountains that cut through southern Morocco. The vast Sahara Desert spilled out on the other side. Taking in the entire scene, I knew that something out there was calling me. I wondered what I would find. Perhaps if I sat under a bodhi tree like the Buddha, or walked over the mountains and through the desert for forty days and nights as Jesus had done, I would discover the answers to the

questions that, on this day, seemed immense and important.

One year later I returned to the camel market, and soon
thereafter I carried out my vision quest, against the advice
of practically everyone I knew. They warned that I would
be killed either by Berbers—the fierce inhabitants of the
High Atlas Mountains—or wild animals, or the rugged terrain and severe weather. Nevertheless, I purchased a donkey to help carry my gear and took off. For three weeks I
journeyed like a nomad, traveling alone on foot across the
mountains and through the punishing desert terrain, covering over three hundred miles. Often hungry and thirsty,
I was determined to maintain the traditional Muslim fast
of Ramadan with its simple rules of no eating, drinking
water, smoking, or sex from sunrise to sunset. My own
monsters kept me company, as well as those I was forced to
encounter in the environment. When I reached the end of
my journey, I checked into a hotel, looking forward to the
luxury of a hot shower and a soft bed. Once in my hotel
room, I was completely startled when I looked into a full-
length mirror. I didn't recognize my body. I was lean; I
looked weak, but I felt strong. The shocking sight of this
new physique brought up all kinds of emotions. *What happened to my body?* Tears of loss became tears of joy as I recognized a healing transformation had taken place. I had
acquired a profound, new inner strength. I felt reborn.

A vision quest is a radical means of getting in touch with
one's deepest self by eliminating the familiar distractions
of daily living and venturing out into the unknown. It is a
spiritual adventure of the purest sort. As a Native American tradition, young men were sent into the wilderness
alone and without provisions for a period of time to test
their bravery and connections with nature; tribal leaders

merged with the isolation of the desert in order to listen intently to the guidance they believed they would hear.

The serious vision-quest initiate takes only the barest of necessities—perhaps a water bottle and a knife—and returns days later with greater understanding of the self and one's place in the world, freed from whatever issues, problems, and dilemmas were uppermost in his life prior to it.

Even now, adventure travel companies and organizations that lead tours to sacred places around the globe offer various versions of a vision-quest experience from mild to fairly intense. For a few days or more than a dozen, one can have the experience of being alone in the desert in the southwest United States, sleeping under the stars, keeping company with none other than one's own being. A fasting regimen is often part of the experience so that the physical body can be cleansed and renewed.

Many backpackers, hikers, and trekkers know the lessons of the experience. Now and then the media reports the story of a lone person who, desperate to get back in touch with the richness in life, takes off on foot or bicycle to cross the country in search of the people, places, and stories that will nourish his soul. Without a doubt, a genuine vision quest is a life-changing experience.

For the modern spiritual adventurer, setting aside the radio, television, fax, laptop computer, and cellular phone for a week may be a good beginning to a vision quest. Instead of daily commuting, one does *daily communing* with the natural world, inviting the true self to express itself without the noise and pressures of daily responsibilities. Retreat centers all across the country offer modest lodging, simple meals, and plenty of time to be alone in nature. While this approach doesn't test life survival skills, it will most likely evoke essential inner responses that seem new and vibrant. Retreating into the quiet of the self to let the soul speak is perhaps the antidote to Thoreau's often quoted commentary that "the mass of men lead lives of quiet desperation."

How to do Go on a Vision Quest

Depending upon the degree of difficulty, *do not attempt your vision quest without plenty of advance preparation.* If you plan a wilderness adventure, research the area, gather maps, and fill your backpack with water, energy bars, a flashlight, matches, and a first-aid kit. If you have special health-related considerations, visit your doctor first. While all of this is good common sense, I can't stress this enough. And there are other important aspects to your preparation. . . .

Form a question that relates to a big issue in your life. Perhaps you are considering a major change such as marriage, divorce, or parenthood; or transplanting yourself in a different part of the country; or looking for a new profession that will satisfy parts of yourself you only rarely glimpse, but now feel compelled to explore and express. It may be that you sense a new spiritual depth is now available to you, and you wish to ignite it with a meaningful experience in solitude. Or you are interested in adding another dimension to a regimen of fasting and meditation that you've been experimenting with. Your intention for a vision quest should be to grasp new truths, inviting clarity, honesty, and an open heart to show you a future filled with unimagined possibilities.

Option One: A day in the park.

On the most basic level, make a commitment to remove yourself from everything that is a reminder of your daily routines for a minimum of one day. If you aren't fasting, pack a light lunch and visit a nearby state park. Ask park rangers to suggest a way to hike or walk their best trails for an entire day in relative solitude. Take along a notebook for capturing insights that surface. If you can afford the time, spend the night in a cabin, tent, or under the stars in your sleeping bag. Don't take books, a radio, or anything else that might distract you from getting in touch with your own inner guidance.

Option Two: Several days.

If you are an experienced camper, add more days to your experience, and have your vision quest in a location you've never visited. For safety considerations, invite a friend to join you and make plans to meet up with that person at several points during the adventure. If you establish a campsite together, agree to have meals in silence.

Option Three: Wilderness outing.

You may feel ready to have "the real thing"—a week or more in the wilderness. Contact travel resources and investigate your options thoroughly. Talk to others who have participated in their wilderness adventures where the vision-quest experience is the primary objective. If you already possess basic survival skills and are fairly confident, choose your location accordingly. Go for it. This is not about sending postcards to your friends and family back home. This is about having a peak experience—transformation through adventure.

> *There is a time in every man's education when he arrives at the conviction that envy is ignorance; that imitation is suicide. . . .* —Ralph Waldo Emerson

Exercise 38. Find Your LifeSport
Monster: Vitality and Longevity

To travel successfully along the freedom path, health and physical fitness are essential, yet maintaining them is certainly not without its monsters. I have asthma. I know what it is like not to be able to breathe easily. While I'm fortunate never to have had any major injuries or other physical problems to severely restrict my activities, I learned long ago that being fit makes everything else in life more enjoyable. Food tastes better. Work is more satisfying. And when it comes to playing and relaxing, the options are far more plentiful. It raises the quality of life like nothing else I know.

Why does exercising require such tremendous effort and motivation? I'm not sure, but the problem is universal. Perhaps we aren't convinced we need to exercise. On a good day we feel fit, and on a bad day we're too tired. Or perhaps we don't like to sweat, strain, and feel the body's resistance to movement. Gravity is a powerful force. The motivation monster is present in many aspects of our lives, but neglecting the needs of our bodies is a huge mistake that most of us will pay for later in life as the effects of aging begin to accumulate and take their toll.

Continuously setting new goals is one way to stay motivated. Making a game of exercise works for some people— assigning ourselves points for certain activities and then periodically cashing them in on a meaningful reward. For example, ten points equals thirty minutes of exercise, and one hundred points means you get to dine at your favorite restaurant or enjoy some other treat that motivates you. There are plenty of creative ways to trick yourself into taking action *now* when you can have a long list of reasons to justify "later is good enough."

The best way, in my opinion, is to discover the fun and joy of exercise by choosing a LifeSport—something we can stay committed to for decades, that becomes richer, more interesting, and more meaningful the longer we do it. Over the years I have witnessed stunning transformations in people who do nothing more than commit to an exercise program *as a way of life* instead of "when time allows." You don't have to be an athlete. Regardless of your age, sex, experience, health limitations, or body type—tall, short, thin, fat, young, old—it just doesn't matter. Whatever condition you are in right this moment, you can begin doing something that will take you to the next level of fitness and health. Finding your LifeSport—something you enjoy doing enough *to do it the rest of your life*—is a discovery well worth the time and effort.

I love swimming, kayaking, and mountain bike riding. Running, however, is one of my favorite LifeSports. While this *Hug the Monster* exercise is devoted to pointing out all the benefits of many potential LifeSports, I want to devote a few sentences to explain why I consider jogging to be such an ideal way to stay in good shape and have lots of fun doing it.

Unlike with many activities, the only equipment required is a great pair of running shoes. There are no court fees, greens fees, or membership dues. Scheduling is a breeze. The great outdoors never closes, so the hours and the wardrobe are completely up to you. And it is portable. When I travel I always bring my running shoes and sweats with me. I've even been known to make laps through airport terminals when the layover is more than an hour. City streets and parks, suburban neighborhoods, beaches, jogging and biking trails, and even back roads are all potential spots for a good, safe, enjoyable run.

The social aspects of running are as rewarding as the opportunities for solitude and clear thinking. For ten straight years, my son Daren and I have joined eighty thousand others, many in outrageous costumes, in a 12K event well known to runners everywhere as the Bay to Breakers. He was only ten years old the first time he entered it. When my daughter, Chelsea, was just seven years old, she became the youngest person in history to complete the Double Dipsea, a rigorous fourteen-mile run from the Pacific Ocean over Mount Tamalpais and back again in Marin County, just on the other side of the Golden Gate Bridge. When Sandy took up jogging she loved it so much, within a year she participated in her first half-marathon. Joined by friends who also enjoy jogging, we enter running events in the Bay Area, never concerned with racing against the stopwatch, always focused on having a good time and topping it off with a ritual brunch. Omelettes and home fries never taste so good as after a 10K run in the company of good friends.

My first serious run was through a traffic jam on the way to the Woodstock Festival in 1969. The highway was a parking lot, and we needed to get to the stage to claim our press passes, so I became a courier with a mission. If the thought of running seems boring or monotonous, get creative and stimulate your imagination, or perhaps create an event or purpose to your journey. I call it adventure running because it takes your body and spirit on an adventure. My first solo marathon was up, over, and mostly down a mountain in Haiti to deliver a note to Papa Doc Duvalier, the Haitian dictator. I love running downhill. When I was denied permission by the Japanese government to skydive into Mount Fuji so that I could run down it, I adjusted my goal. I climbed up and ran back down. The highest mountain in Australia is Mount Kosciusko. At 7,300 feet high it is a rather easy climb; I decided to "Run to the Top of Downunder." The last thirteen kilometers were through a snowfield, making it a unique and especially memorable run.

The case needs to be made that a LifeSport doesn't have to be a grind. It should be something that feels more like fun than work. Sure, some days the motivation to exercise might be hard to muster. But when you can really fall in love with something, it has a far greater chance of becoming a LifeSport. In my experience, these fitness monsters hug you back every time you embrace one. The payoff is both immediate and longer term.

Tennis, golf, aerobics, dance, power walking, biking, skiing, in-line skating . . . they are all candidates for a LifeSport. Cardiovascular exertion is essential. You've got to sweat a little, but just about any activity, when done for a minimum of thirty minutes at a time, is bound to give you an adequate workout. Although researchers can't seem to agree on the ideal type and amount of exercise most of us need, my own experience is clear. Moderate daily workouts are essential, combined with something more rigorous several times a month. For fitness, a sense of accomplishment, and longevity, I am convinced that regular exercise must become as big a priority in our lives as a good healthy diet, adequate sleep, and making love.

How to do Find Your LifeSport

The monster is the degree to which you are imprisoned by lack of energy and vitality, and haunted by good intentions that never pan out. When you feel sluggish, over-

weight, or sleepy, the Inertia Monsters may be lurking behind your easy chair, so just invite them to join you. *Your
goal is to select a fitness activity and stick with it for an entire
month.* What did you love doing as a kid? Perhaps you'll
find some clues to choosing a LifeSport in those memories.
Once accomplished, extend the goal to two months, then
three. Eventually, exercise will be so integrated, you won't
want to live another week without it. When the five-step
method is applied here, you'll be on a learning curve bound
to take you into the sunshine and fresh air, and toward
more fun, better health, and a longer life.

Step One: For couch potatoes.

Walk two miles with a buddy. Today. Pick up the phone
right now and make the call. Do it. No excuses. Set the VCR
to record your favorite program if that's the issue. See how
great you feel when you get home, and ask yourself the
rhetorical question, "Why don't I do this every day?"

Step Two: For fair-weather walkers.

If you can walk for your fitness workout, chances are
that you can jog a little, too. Hug the Monster and find out.
If bad knees or back/spine problems prevent jogging,
make sure your walking program is vigorous enough to
work up a sweat, that you put in at least thirty minutes,
and that you do it a minimum of three times a week. Create
a thirty-day calendar and make it more interesting by
marking your exercise days with insights, observations,
best times, or other details like how many dogs you saw,
the names of new acquaintances, or the various types of
flowers growing along your path. The key to a LifeSport is
stimulation, interest, and fun in addition to fitness.

Step Three: For active exercisers.

Maybe you attend aerobics classes regularly, but you don't really enjoy them. Or perhaps you put your time in on the treadmill or stair-stepping machine, while hating it the entire time. *Find the thing you love to do.* If you haven't yet found your LifeSport but are fairly fit, you engage in moderate workouts already, and want to expand your options, here's a suggestion: Do something new once a week for several months. See how many different ways of exercising you can add to your total experience, and in the process, discover some that you could fall in love with. Try yoga. In-line skating. Join a volleyball team. Or go power walking. Swim. Play racquetball. Experiment, and play with your pals like ten-year-olds.

If you want to expand this step, create a point system. Accumulate points for each exercise session and come up with a list of meaningful rewards. Invite a buddy to join you in your quest for your LifeSport and celebrate your small victories together. Take a good look around your community for clubs and associations, classes and free demonstrations. While a total fitness program also includes strength-building and stretching, *the characteristics of an excellent life sport are:* cardiovascular workout, social aspects, convenience, cost, flexibility and ease of scheduling, weather restrictions, portability, availability of equipment and courses, skill levels, and most of all, fun.

> *If it doesn't absorb you, if it isn't any fun, don't do it.*
> —D.H. Lawrence

Exercise 39. Passages
Monster: No Growth

The San Francisco Bay and I have been through a lot together. The day I turned sixteen, I competed in a long-distance swimming race in the Bay from Pier Seven to Treasure Island. I almost drowned. I was a sprinter on the high
school swim team and wasn't prepared for either the distance or the severity of the cold water. Fierce leg cramps
immobilized me and started to take me down. Miraculously, a Coast Guard boat veered in and scooped me up
under the Bay Bridge just before my last swallow. Ten years
later, on my twenty-sixth birthday, better prepared and
staunchly determined, I swam the Golden Gate for the first
time. Unlike my first experience in the Bay, this swim
would radically change my life.

On October 17, 1989, drawn once again by the heartbeat
of the Bay, I elected to celebrate my birthday and my
twenty-fifth anniversary as an adventurer by kayaking
from the Golden Gate Bridge to Candlestick Park, where
the Giants were hosting the Oakland A's for game three of
the World Series. I had recently begun my new career as a
public speaker and I outwardly acknowledged it as another rite of passage. It seemed only right to seek a blessing
from the Bay, especially on a day the whole town was already in the mood to celebrate due to the "Bridge to
Bridge" World Series.

Although I had estimated four hours for the fifteen-mile
kayak journey, swift flood tides carried me in two hours
and fifteen minutes. In between traffic reports, news heli-
copters reported my progress as "the hometown adventurer who had discovered the fastest route to Candlestick."
At noon, when I pulled my kayak onto the shore, reporters

descended on me like seagulls, hungry to have a fresh angle on the baseball story. A camera crew shot footage that they said was for Dan Rather's CBS network evening newscast. For me, it would have been a real topper of a birthday present. But at 5:04 P.M., thousands of lives changed forever when a 7.1 earthquake struck the city. I was sitting in commuter traffic on Highway 101, heading to Sacramento to give a speech, when it hit. It felt like a blowout until the car started moving again and radio reports told us what no San Franciscan wanted to know. . . . the Bay Bridge had collapsed and people were killed; the Marina District was on fire; power was out everywhere. The damage reports were chaotic and chilling.

People think I'm fearless. I'm not. I definitely feel fear, but I have learned through experience how to manage it. No matter how threatening an external event appears to be, the biggest monsters are always inside ourselves. My children were one hundred miles away in Santa Cruz, about fifteen miles from the quake's epicenter. With roads closed and phones out, I endured fourteen hours of fear and worry through countless aftershocks until I heard from their mother the next morning that their only loss was the brick chimney. But it had been a very long night waiting for the good news.

Rites of passage inform our lives with meaning. If there is a singular message the Bay is offering to teach me, perhaps it is that the mere fact of living here, or anywhere else for that matter, is a risk worth taking. And that mastering nature anywhere is not the point. Rather, through nature, we can learn to master ourselves.

Sometimes we change our lives; other times life changes us. Even seemingly small events can trigger big changes. But a rite of passage is only symbolically represented by the external event. *An opening in our awareness is the essence of the event's true significance, because in that moment we die and are reborn.* In the same instant we realize that the limited self must be expanded, we may be seeing the so-called "limit" for the very first time as we cast it off. This process is easy to see in nature—caterpillar into butterfly, autumn leaves and new spring growth, the snake shedding its skin. The entire cycle of life is captured in four words: birth, growth, death, renewal. In this sense, rites of passage are like seasons appearing at unknown intervals.

Perhaps we can not experience the fullness of our lives except in the blossoming of awareness in the present moment. When we grow, perhaps we don't even really change, we just become more authentic versions of ourselves . . . more of what we are, less of what we are not. It is an interesting philosophical question filled with paradox. Rites of passage are markers that fill us with meaning, direction, and context for additional learning and growth.

How to do Passages

Phase One: The past.

Which events in your life turned out to be rites of passage? Leaving home, marriage, divorce, the birth of a child, the death of someone important in your life, your first job, completing a college degree—these are the obvious candidates. But go a little deeper with the question. What moments stand out in which an insight or expanded awareness altered your concept of yourself and your potential? Are there times in your past when clarity finally formed from confusion and chaos? Did you reach a moment in your maturity where you ultimately accepted yourself, the good along with the bad? In a forgiving act, did you experience a greater capacity for love and compassion that reframed your values? What about life goals? Perhaps you can map your life from these rites of passage.

Here's the exercise: You are going to create your own Map of Passages. Make a list of all the passages that have come to your mind while reading this exercise. Note your age, what people were involved, the circumstances, and how you changed. Then transfer this information to a timeline so you can look at it in a glance, leaving plenty of room for adding new entries as they occur to you. Once you start looking for moments of major growth in your life, you'll remember others. With the map fairly complete, look for patterns. Perhaps your passages have similar themes that may be clues to your special life talents, gifts, and lessons, and perhaps they will reveal the picture of someone with greater potential than your current self-image allows. Use this exercise as a time of growth through reflection.

Phase Two: Future passages.

As we mature, we realize that we can take charge of our growth far more than we could as children and adolescents. Use the same Map of Passages timeline concept. Extend a line into the future from one year to as many as fifty—whatever you are comfortable with. Place events, issues, goals, or meaningful questions along the line and imagine what may be required to incorporate them into your greater self. This may take large doses of imagination, faith, hope—whatever words you assign to your potential, harness them. Then know that, with sustained effort, your skills at monster hugging will positively effect your ability to have the life you really want. You may find it useful to review the warm-up exercises again, either to transfer dreams and fears to the timeline, or because you want to add a few new dreams and fears to your original lists.

Phase Three: Rebirthday.

In this phase, we want to suggest that you find an event and a date to celebrate annually that symbolizes a moment of rebirth. It may be a birthday or anniversary, but it could just as easily be something far less conventional. Perhaps it is the date you moved to a new city. Or earned your certification. Or an otherwise ordinary day that became extraordinary because of an awareness you gained, a kindness you bestowed or received, or a place you visited that made you feel special. Perhaps you acted bravely and overcame tremendous obstacles. If the day is worthy of the name Rebirthday, it is worthy of celebration. This is a holiday in your honor. Begin planning how you will spend the day when it next rolls around on the calendar. Whether it is a quiet day of reflection walking in the park or a boisterous party with lots of friends doesn't matter. The point is that you honor yourself and your growth in a way that expresses just how special you are, and how hard-earned your growth has been. This is a practice that can continue to grow in meaning over the years, a wonderful gift to give yourself. If it feels right, teach this technique to your children, too. Pass it on.

> *Men stumble over the truth from time to time, but*
> *most pick themselves up and hurry off as if nothing*
> *happened.*   —Winston Churchill

Exercise 40. Never Give Up
Monster: Justifying Barriers

People often ask me, "What is the most difficult adventure you've ever done?" I can't easily single out one. Just about every major adventure was the most difficult. By making a career of pushing my own limits, necessity demanded that I develop a certain expertise in recognizing the difference between authentic limitations and temporary setbacks, between energizing self-confidence and debilitating self-doubt. The degree of difficulty is a matter of perspective and hindsight, and can be measured by how many opportunities there are to bail out along the way.

Swimming from Africa to Europe, kayaking the Nile, trekking the Sahara, jumping into the Mayan Well of Sacrifice, any number of triathlons and marathons . . . you name the adventure and I can tell you about the moments where giving up was more than a slight temptation, and even totally justifiable. When I made a commitment to complete my college degrees, I was in my early forties and the father of two young toddlers. My wife, a flight attendant, was away several days at a time. Halfway through the last semester, I didn't think I could do it all. Yet, dropping some classes meant delaying graduation; doing too much meant perhaps missing my goal of finishing summa cum laude. More recently, as an inexperienced public speaker, a few uncomfortable performances was all it took for me to wonder why I ever thought it was a good career move.

Accepting and meeting each of those challenges has always meant facing the probability that somewhere along the line a little voice will whisper in my ear, "Bail out now, pal. It's okay. You've given it your best shot. No one expects you to do more. Take a break." By definition, pushing the limits means hitting the wall. And when the wall is in plain sight, the brain gets busy explaining all the reasons why getting out *now* is the best thing to do. Learning to override those messages and persevere to the end is central to the art and adventure of hugging monsters.

Peaks and valleys are part of life, no matter what we're attempting. The highs and lows are predictable. To a certain degree, we can prepare for them with practice, learning to pace ourselves, and giving permission to take little timeouts. But when intense discomfort begs us to reconsider the goal, we have to rely on something else to keep going. If we don't, temporary amnesia sets in. Forgetting our original inspiration, we rationalize, justify, and explain how the goal has lost its meaning. The barriers are too numerous, the pain is too great, and the sacrifice isn't worth it. What is that something else? It's called a *second wind*.

In endurance sports, a second wind is a predictable physiological phenomenon that occurs when the body's natural pharmacy manufactures and releases that which is needed to rise to the occasion. Highly trained elite marathon runners don't often experience "hitting the wall" because they train accordingly and develop the physiological and psychological skills needed to get them to the finish line. In other words, they know how to factor a second wind into their performance. We can learn to do the same.

Second wind is a useful metaphor that can be applied to anything that challenges us beyond a certain level. It is an aspect of self-mastery. In life as well as in sport, when a second wind kicks in, we are rewarded with everything we need to get to the next step . . . and the next, and the next. Energy and essential resources appear. Our sense of time alters and the pace is perfect. Optimism returns. The goal now seems within reach again. We know we can make it to the end. Experiencing the second wind, we are renewed. We no longer doubt that the journey is worth every ache, pain, and negative thought that carried us to that moment. Trusting the arrival of a second wind is a matter of practice and experience.

We should always give ourselves credit for any amount of effort we put forth when it comes to moving toward meaningful goals and making changes in our lives. Every event doesn't have to be the equivalent of a marathon. That's not what I'm saying here. But in fact, when we find ourselves in a marathon of some kind—a huge commitment that tests our limits—what price do we pay for giving up? For not burning the midnight oil to meet a deadline? For not saving money in the way we promised? For breaking a diet at the ten-pound mark instead of going for the fifteen we originally intended? For doing a mediocre job on a proposal instead of our very best effort? For walking away from a relationship instead of doing the hard work? For *settling*?

Each of us must decide for ourselves and find a way to live with the choice of how much is enough. Often, if we don't get to the second wind, we'll get a second chance somewhere else along the line where perhaps the lessons and the experience are slightly different. But the lesson in *Never Give Up* is contained in the awesome satisfaction that comes at the end. We just can't know it till we get there. Like children batting at a Mexican piñata until one final blow makes it burst, we are showered with rewards beyond our ability to imagine them. The banality of Yogi Berra's famous quip that "It ain't over till it's over" is also profound. Begin as many times as you must. Never, ever, ever give up.

How to do Never Give Up

We aren't as free as we could be until we know we can go the full distance . . . until we rely on a second wind as second nature. Just about everything in life boils down to motivation. To the degree we have enough, even the most difficult tasks are enjoyable. At the start of a new venture, we gather information, fine-tune our skills, and look forward to the future when the goal will be realized. The relationship is filled with fireworks and excitement. The new job feels like a million bucks. When the school semester begins, the notebooks are fresh, the pencils are sharpened, and the clothes are new. At the grand opening celebration, the shop's windows and floors sparkle; the shelves are brimming with neatly arranged merchandise. Eventually arguments surface in the relationship, your boss becomes Scrooge, midterm exams are fast approaching, and the now dull store windows stop attracting customers. What the heck happened?

Phase One: Review your achievement patterns.

Do you have the tendency to start things and never finish them? Do you hang on too long? Which of your accomplishments fill you with pride and why? Where in your experience did a second wind show up? What kind of support structure do you typically operate with? Are you often impatient and expedient, cutting corners when a longer route is in order? Reflect on the very best moments in your life when you felt rewarded for doing a difficult thing. Recall the process and the people involved. From all of this reflection, determine your patterns, and whether or not you have work to do.

Phase Two: Make a commitment.

If you've ever tried to swing a golf club, tennis racket, or baseball bat, you know that accuracy and distance depend on a good follow-through in the swing. Many of us have the tendency to have a great windup and an incomplete follow-through. It is something that requires diligent attention, practice, and concentration.

What one accomplishment could you successfully complete within the next three months with a sustained effort? Use it as your focal point for this exercise. Make a commitment to crossing the finish line with it. Define what success looks like. Set your parameters and gauge your expectations accordingly. To lose weight. To be able to run five miles without walking a single step. To go after a promotion at work. To write a business plan and secure the financing. To finish your novel. To complete five other *Hug the Monster* exercises. Share this commitment with at least one person. Follow the five-step method. Set the date. Begin and don't stop.

> *If at first you don't succeed, something is blocking your way.* —Michael Ray

Exercise 41. Masai Stand
Monster: Staying Grounded

Although they are warriors, when the Masai are tending their cattle in the plains of East Africa, you'd be hard-pressed to find a more pastoral and peaceful scene. Their tall, lean, dark bodies appear silhouetted against the burning sun, and produce a striking, unforgettable image. The job requires that they remain alert to possible predators, yet relaxed enough to maintain their watch for long hours. They've discovered a way of standing that apparently yields the desired result. They stand on one leg with the other leg nestled into their thigh just above the knee, using their long spears for extra balance.

On the banks of the Ganges River in the foothills of the Himalayas, I have seen holy men, called sadhus, meditating in this same posture, uncannily maintaining balance and poise without using a stick or spear. Masai warriors and Indian sadhus have very little else in common, yet they each suggest there is something we can learn about using the body as a focal point for generating an alert, calm, centered feeling.

I have practiced this way of standing, and find it to be very useful for quickly achieving a sense of inner balance. Hatha yoga offers a similar posture. Freedom to be fully present in the moment sometimes means setting our cares aside long enough to experience reconnecting with our bodies. Ironically, the physical symptoms of high anxiety and stress are often the result of being too much in our heads. Instead of blowing a fuse, here are two quick and easy exercises for getting grounded and peaceful again.

How to do the Masai Stand

Part One: Balance and breathe.

When first learning this, feel free to use something for balance—a wall, the edge of a table, or a broom handle. In a comfortable standing position, raise your right foot and place it inside your left thigh, toes pointing toward the floor. If you can't raise it that high, rest it on your calf or knee, but make sure your right foot rests snugly against your leg. To help establish your balance, fix your eyesight on something ten feet or more in front of you. Once you are balanced, let go of your support. Press your palms together and bring them to your heart as if praying. Breathe long and deep, holding the posture for a minute, focusing your awareness into your body. Change legs and repeat the posture. You may find it is easier to stand on one leg than the other. Each time you practice this, extend the length of time you can hold the stance to create balance, grounding, and inner peace for yourself.

Part Two: More grounding.

Follow the Masai Stand with this exercise and you will deepen the grounding process. Place your feet shoulders' width apart and slowly bend your knees, moving into a squatting position, keeping your feet flat on the floor. Adjust the angle of your feet if necessary, but keep them flat, especially your heels, while you go as far into a squat as you can. Let your arms fall to a comfortable position inside your knees. Breathe deeply into your belly and release as much tension as possible, letting it all fall to the bottom of your feet. Now stand erect slowly, paying special attention to the bottom of your feet and your thighs as you rise. This exercise stimulates energy in the lower body. Like the Masai Stand, it adds a new sense of balance and grounding.

Because these exercises don't take a lot of time, they are especially valuable as a stress-management technique. Just close the door, remove your shoes, and in a few minutes you'll feel more in control again, ready to tackle the next meeting or task with greater clarity.

Be the change you are trying to create. —Gandhi

Exercise 42. White-water Rafting
Monster: Outrageous Fun

On the chance that reading about my outdoor adventures is starting to inspire you to have a few of your own, here's one almost anyone can do regardless of physical fitness and skill level. White-water rafting sounds thrilling and difficult. Only the thrill part is accurate.

I introduced my children to white-water rafting when Daren was eight and Chelsea was only five. At the end of the first raft trip both kids were crying. Chelsea's tears were over the possibility that we would do it again, and Daren's were for if we didn't. It was a precious beginning to what has become a favorite family sport. Since then we've run wild rivers many times in northern California and through Costa Rican rain forests. The children's comfort in the water has allowed us to expand to kayaking adventures along the Danube River in Austria and Hungary, as well as in the San Francisco Bay, the Gulf of Mexico, and the Pacific Ocean. More recently, Daren and I ran two rain forest rivers in

Costa Rica with the triple thrill of class-five rapids, breathtaking scenery, and a father-son experience loaded with bonding, intensity, and our own special memories.

I'm not suggesting that you buy a raft and hit the river. There are plenty of river-running companies throughout the world ready and willing to take you on the ride of your life without any previous experience. Trained guides are in charge of everything. They explain all of the safety rules and paddling instructions, and after a quick demonstration you're off! The guides do 95 percent of the steering. Rapids are rated on a scale from one to seven—little ripples to suicide runs—and most beginners can easily handle threes and fours with plenty of excitement. Popular outdoor magazines carry directories of white-water river companies. When you request a few brochures, you'll learn what to wear, bring, and expect. You'll also become more familiar with the rating system, and you can select your destination accordingly. On many of the more popular rivers, photographers sit on the banks adjacent to big rapids ready to capture your expression in the midst of a thriller. By the time you are dry and enjoying your picnic lunch at the end of the run, the film is printed and ready to be purchased as proof of your big adventure.

How to do White-water Rafting

This is a very affordable adventure. Get some brochures by checking the classified advertising section of popular outdoor magazines. You may want to consider finding a river close to home to make it a weekend trip in the car. Once you have a river in mind, talk it over with a few friends. Estimate the budget, compare calendars, and set the date. Depending on your destination, the experience can be intense, producing a valuable bond between everyone in the group. Perhaps you can include a raft trip in your next family reunion, or make it a team-building exercise for a core group of folks at work. For the small amount of effort and expense, the payoff in outrageous fun is astronomical. The only sore muscles you may experience will be in your face from laughing and grinning so much, and you'll probably be planning your next trip before the raft is pulled back onto the shore.

> *I asked a very successful friend at our twenty-fifth alumni reunion of the Harvard Business School for his measure of success. He said, "I learned to smell the roses."*
> —Robert Medearis

Exercise 43. *Do You Wanna Dance?*
Monster: Nothing to Celebrate

The Long Distance Swimmer that Trains in a Discotheque" was the headline on the cover of *Life* magazine in Australia after I swam Africa to Europe a second time. I love to dance. As a kid, I took dance lessons and never looked back. For me, dancing is all about getting in touch with a rhythm. It's also about connecting, celebrating, having fun, and feeling free. I once had an experience in which the connection was unusual and intense, but it wasn't on any ordinary dance floor in a disco. . . .

I was in Haiti on a running adventure when I met the French photographer Catherine Leroy, a five-foot-tall, ninety-five-pound dynamo with a legendary reputation for getting her story in the way Eliot Ness always got his man.

Two *Life* magazine reporters told me how she challenged and overpowered marine officers; her face still bore the shrapnel scars she suffered while working in North Vietnam, where she was eventually taken prisoner. "Hell on wheels" would not be an overstatement. In Haiti, she was on assignment for an Italian magazine as well as *Look*, doing two photo stories, one on the Haitian CIA, and the other on voodoo. After we met, she expressed interest in covering my solo marathon run there. Her investigation into Haitian voodoo generated an invitation to attend an authentic voodoo ceremony, which she in turn extended to me and my film crew. We accepted on the spot.

The wood shack was outside of Port-au-Prince. The room was starkly furnished. A beat-up old wooden table was covered with crosses, beads, incense, voodoo dolls, a couple of half-full whiskey bottles, and dried flowers draping the corners. Small rickety wooden benches lined the walls. In one corner of the room, three men in soiled, perspiration-soaked white shirts stood beating the tops of conga drums. There wasn't a seat available when the four of us entered, but they made room anyway. We squeezed in. Things were just starting to roll. About forty people—more women than men—were present, but there was very little relating going on. A few got up to dance.

Looking around, I saw that many people were dressed in white. The voodoo priest, called a *houngan,* wore a white shirt and a '40s style Bogart hat. Taking a swig of whiskey, he singled out a young woman standing in the corner and put his hand on her head. At his touch, she recoiled, trembled, and shook a moment, then screamed. The four of us dove for our cameras.

A dozen or so Haitians were now moving to the drums, and the room smelled of smoke and sweat. The voodoo priestess, known as the *mambo,* wore a simple white dress. A white bandanna covered her hair. She gracefully glided around the room touching people, mesmerizing them as she passed. The drumming intensified. All at once a bolt from the drum hit me in the solar plexus. I felt a force lift me right off the bench. Simultaneous with that, the *mambo* appeared in front of me, inviting me to dance. Later, the reports of my dancing and gyrating as observed by Catherine and my film crew included amazement that I had behaved as someone who was possessed. I can't fully explain what happened, but I know the drums, the *mambo,* and the setting contributed to an unforgettable, powerfully eerie experience.

How to do Do You Wanna Dance?

Part One: With yourself.

Next time you are home alone and feeling the need to connect with and energize yourself, dance for a half an hour or so. You may feel silly at first if you've never done this, but that's okay. It will pass as soon as you let yourself *feel into* your body's natural desire to move. Whether you boogie to Elton John or pirouette to Stravinsky, move around the room freely. Let your arms, legs, and torso express the stored-up emotions words can't get to. This is a great way to spend an overload of anxiety, as well as to turn a slight depression into a brighter, more balanced outlook.

Part Two: With others.

Do you enjoy dancing but can't find a partner who also does? Or is social dancing one of those things that keeps you from accepting invitations to parties because you never learned how? Did you take tap and ballet as a little kid and wonder why you didn't keep it up as an adult? If the film *Dirty Dancing* is among your all-time favorites, but you've only fantasized about dancing in that way, now is the time to make it real. If it's in your soul, you owe it to yourself to find it in your body, too.

Take dance lessons. Ballroom. Tap. Jazz. Aerobic dancing. It's all fantastic. You'll meet people who also love to dance. You'll gain new confidence, expand your social horizons, and have loads of fun. Your community is full of resources. Get busy. You can make it happen this month if you want to. Do you wanna dance? Yes!

Celebrate, celebrate, dance to the music!
—Three Dog Night

Chapter Seven

The Eternal Monsters

Eternal Monsters exert a steady but often unrecognized presence in our lives. Yet even when felt, they can go un-named for years. Perhaps inseparable from the life-force it-self, they are the energy of our personalities, the light in our eyes, and the fire in our bellies. Our familiarity with Eternal Monsters can be gauged in many ways. For exam-ple, the ease with which we laugh and cry, the ways we deal with pain when we experience loss, the peacefulness with which we encounter solitude, and the compassion that connects us to the rest of the world may each suggest our degree of previous exposure to Eternal Monsters. Whether confronted with the most complex or the simplest issues in life, embracing the Eternal Monsters seems to be nature's sublime reward for being human. Hugging them, while difficult, can be a transcendent experience.

Why me? Why here? Why now? are the three questions that most readily awaken sleeping Eternal Monsters, especially when the questions are unconditional and we want to know the truth. The awesome despair that can accompany personal tragedy frequently brings up these monsters. When illness, death, emotional trauma, or severe material loss touches us, we know we will be changed by the experience, but in our humanness we are uncertain as to exactly how. For better? Or for worse?

Such experiences shock us into a view of life that, at least momentarily, feels hostile to our security and well-being. Dark clouds hover over us. We are numb. We wonder, *will life ever be sweet again?* When the Eternal Monsters are working their purpose in our lives, we feel their effects in the core of our being. We feel more than just a little down, dissatisfied, or unsettled. Our sadness is profound as we face the mysteries of life, unable and ill-equipped to answer the questions that have surfaced like aliens into our waking consciousness. Generally, we proceed according to our instincts. Directly or indirectly, nature does the healing at varying speeds, perhaps more slowly if we are not active participants in the healing process. If we choose to hug the monsters for everything they are worth, not only will our healing be more rapid, but more importantly, it will be transforming.

The Eternal Monsters are also concerned with the quality of our awareness, our intentions, and the meaning and purpose we assign to life's daily pleasures, irritations, and challenges. They cycle through our lives at various watershed periods and ask us to re-examine our direction and to dispel myths and beliefs that no longer serve our growth. They suggest, by their very presence, that we must find another, more satisfying way to live. They remind us that time is precious, that we are here for a purpose, and that our quest is none other than to fulfill that purpose.

The Inertia and Logic Monsters are hugged by moving our awareness out of our heads and into our hearts. Relationship and Freedom Monsters urge us to be active, engaging, playful, and courageous participants in our own lives. The Eternal Monsters are most directly connected to our spirits. Hugging them means tapping into the sacred ground within our being—however we may comprehend it—and confronting the unknown.

Eternal Monsters are universally felt in the human species, and perhaps organized religion is our most obvious response to their presence. Yet they seem to be more available to us outside of any particular dogma or structure. Eternal Monsters must be experienced, not merely thought about. To hug them we must be willing to suspend *what we think we know* and explore our depths freely and without judgment. It is quite possible that some of the most fulfilled people on Earth are those who have intimate first-hand experience with the Eternal Monsters.

Although we commonly encounter them under painful circumstances, it isn't necessary to be in a crisis in order to meet our Eternal Monsters. On the contrary, meeting them on purpose is excellent preparation for managing life's future difficulties. When we have learned to trust life even in small measure, we are prepared to step up to the Eternal Monsters and with a hug, ask, "Now what?" Their gifts are like a rudder that guides us, or a compass that points a direction where it was previously unseen. From them we gain a greater sense of our own meaning, purpose, and potential . . . one layer, one question, one hug at a time. Though they reside in darkness, they are the champions of the divine light within each of us.

Exercise 44. *Sunrise, Sunset*
Monster: Feeling Stranded

When the sun sets in Morocco, swirling orange mixes with shimmering pearl gray and it looks like candy or sherbet. You can almost taste it. The next sunset offers endless shades of purple. Nature has such a wonderful palette. The settling sun makes a silent silhouette . . . connecting temples and churches with giraffes, trees, women balancing pottery on their heads going to and from water wells, a single sail along the water, a glistening, cold, snow-capped peak in the distance . . . all set off in the center of an orange ball. It is spectacular.

Sandy and I woke up early to experience the holy Indian city of Benares coming to life along the Ganges River where Hindus perform their morning rituals. The humble wooden rowboat seemed as old as the city in the dim morning as we climbed in, our guide promising we would be rewarded for our perfectly timed arrival ahead of the sun. As both tourists and expectant pilgrims that morning, we shivered in the chilly predawn air and watched with wonder as the famous scene slowly materialized, a page of *National Geographic* coming to life, and us in it.

As we quietly glided on the river, the view of the left bank offered us the ancient Benares skyline with its curious domed temples and mixed architectural styles; in front of it, the atmosphere was blotted with the perpetual dark smoke and ash of open-air crematoriums. The steady funeral fires were the only detectable light in the grayness of the morning. In stark contrast, the right bank, a flat, delta-like shore with nothing on it, offered the promise of sunrise against the deep indigo sky. The horizon line between the land and the river opened, giving way to daybreak. . . .

First there was a suggestion of light, then an orange halo appeared, and finally, the perfect round sun sat for a moment on the horizon, then majestically lifted itself above the river, casting an orange-pink glow to the left bank, where along the shore Hindu pilgrims were praying, bathing, brushing their teeth, swimming, and washing clothes. Experiencing the sunrise, it was easy to understand why Benares is considered one of India's most sacred spots.

There's a long, white, wooden pier that juts out from a popular spot on a beach near Tampa, Florida. When the sun began to set, all of the activity on the beach stopped and people grew very quiet. Dancing, volleyball, frisbee, splashing in the waves, sand-castle construction—everything came to an amazingly fast halt, and all eyes focused reverently on the pinpoint of the pier where the sun dropped, and the sky became a Monet canvas with a million shades of pink, coral, and purple. No one moved until the sky was dark, except perhaps to cuddle in more closely to one another, offering warmth in the chilly evening air. What a treat for the senses—a benediction without words.

How many sunrises and sunsets have you experienced? Do you know of a special place where you can go right now to catch the morning sun sneaking a peek over the horizon? Will you see plains and meadows? Or rooftops? Or can the orange-red ball of light be framed by trees? Or mountain peaks?

How about watching the sun dropping into a serene, still lake, or into the ocean while you hear the waves crashing, the foam gurgling, pebbles rubbing and crackling together, a symphony of the sea? From your perch, you wonder how it is possible there are so many variations of yellow, orange, red, violet, purple, and pink before night invades and brushes the canvas deep blue, then black, and speckles it with silver starlight and a delicate crescent moon. A chill knocks you out of your reverie, and it is time to leave the wondrous setting. When will you return?

How to do Sunrise, Sunset

Promise yourself both a sunrise and a sunset this week. Don't have any other agenda when you go. Leave your expectations at home. Just have the experience. Let it happen. Repeat it as often as you like. Being mindful of the eternal rising and setting, your own place in the sun can't help but feel right, too.

> *There is a great miracle in listening when there is no*
> *interpretation of what you are hearing. . . . If you listen*
> *with your heart, with care, with attention, then that very*
> *listening is like a flowering.* —J. Krishnamurti

Exercise 45. *"Wherever You Go, There You Are"*
Monster: Staying in the Moment

I was trekking down the south side of the High Atlas Mountains overlooking the Sahara Desert, alone with my donkey, when I was suddenly ambushed by a tough-looking Berber who appeared out of nowhere. I quickly asked to take his picture and handed him a coin, but he wasn't interested. He wanted all of my money, not a token coin. When I grabbed to take the coin back he lunged for me, furious. Sensing immediate danger, instinct took over and instead of responding with a fight, I harmonized with his energy. In one sequence of movements, like a dance, I gave him the coin again, handed him my donkey prodding stick, and invited him with a head gesture and my body language to walk with me toward the desert. He did. I recognized that staying in the purity of the moment could be very powerful and physically empowering. Later, I learned it was a pure aikido move, a martial art that involves learning to harmonize energies, although I had never been exposed to aikido before. It was one of my more amazing experiences in hugging a potentially life-threatening monster.

There's nothing like traveling through multiple time zones in a single day to remind me of the truth in this handy phrase: *Wherever you go, there you are.* Jon Kabat-Zinn wrote a terrific best-selling meditation book by that title, published in 1994. Great truths are simple insights more often than not. Bite-sized wisdom is easy to digest as food for the spirit, and small bites can have profound and nourishing effects. Monsters travel with us regardless of our destinations. They rarely, if ever, agree to stay at home. Personal growth is incremental. The progress can be so slow sometimes, the events that contribute to it can appear to be insignificant. If you've been living your life in search of the one, big, ultimate truth that will instantly transform your life, look again. The Dalai Lama, one of contemporary society's most schooled and respected religious leaders, and one who can wax eloquently for days on the complex elements of Tibetan Buddhism, nevertheless consistently reduces his message to this: "My religion is kindness." This is a simple yet profound statement. What a wise man he is.

How to do "Wherever You Go, There You Are"

Part One: Practice a method of self-inquiry.

I learned this by studying the life of an Indian saint named Ramana Maharshi, who gave the world a simple yet challenging method for being in the present moment.

He named it the Method of Self-Inquiry. To practice his method, the question "Who am I?" is a frame through which you experience yourself in your daily activities, especially those that have a certain intensity to them. When we are mostly in our heads *thinking,* we are actually in the past or the future, and not the present moment. A quality of being in the present moment is the refreshing lack of chattering and judging going on inside.

When you are happy, sad, working hard, relaxing, or doing the dishes in the kitchen—any activity you can name, any emotion you are feeling—pose the question, Who am I? For example, "Who is being rejected?" "Who is crying?" "Who is bewildered?" "Who is losing her temper at her children?" and so on. You may develop a calm inner sense of being that grows stronger and clearer as you work with the exercise, learning to detect and eliminate the blathering and noise in your head that can steal your peace of mind. Try it for a week and see if this is a method that works for you.

Part Two: Learn to meditate.

Contrary to popular notions about meditation, it isn't difficult and there aren't a lot of rules. There are many ways to meditate, and plenty of methods to explore. The only goal of meditation is focused awareness and the experience of being totally present. A great meditation session is when no part of you is back at the office rehashing yesterday's meeting, or projecting into the future, planning Thanksgiving dinner. In meditation, active thinking stops. The thoughts may continue to stream through like cars in rush-hour traffic, but they have no real attraction to hold you. You don't hop in, but rather stay on the side of the road watching them pass by, so to speak. Meditation gets easier with familiarity and practice. Beginners are often filled with various forms of, *Nothing's happening. Am I doing this right?* If that's your question, chances are you are doing it exactly right.

With sustained practice, you'll soon learn to look forward to the benefits of meditation. Some of those benefits are the feeling of being reenergized, centered, and clear in your thinking. Depending upon the depth of your experience and your intentions, you may also emerge from a meditation session with a peaceful, more spiritual connection to everything and everyone around you. But don't start out with that in mind or you may be setting yourself up for a huge disappointment.

Some people like performing rituals and repeating mantras. Others have learned that a walk in the park is sufficient. Your goal is to enjoy a quiet mind without *trying* to create one. A more detailed description of a meditative practice called *progressive relaxation* is included with Exercise 46, *A Special Place to Relax*. The following is an ideal way to begin learning the dynamics of basic meditation.

If you've always wanted to learn to meditate, commit yourself to this: Each day for a week, claim fifteen minutes in a relaxing, quiet place where you won't be disturbed. Close your eyes. Begin by noticing your breathing. Without being too self-conscious or "trying" to hard, feel into your body as you inhale and exhale. See how relaxed you can make yourself. Be aware of how you feel in your stomach, your face, your shoulders. If you sense tension, let it go. If your thoughts are moving by too quickly, and you can't stop thinking about work or your busy to-do list, imagine a peaceful scene and lose yourself in it. Treat thoughts like clouds in the sky and don't make one more important than another. When your time has ended, don't be surprised if colors seem a bit brighter, sounds are clearer, and you feel refreshed in a pleasant way. Sit for a moment or two longer, eyes open, and reflect on how it felt. Remember those sensations, and when you next practice meditating, call them to mind. You'll enter your meditative state of being a little more easily each time you practice.

> *So, in meditation practice, the best way to get somewhere is to let go of trying to get anywhere at all.*—Jon Kabat-Zinn

Exercise 46. A Special Place to Relax
Monster: Stress

Vivid mental images of naturally beautiful settings can generate inner calm almost instantly. It is as if our spirits are so eager to commune with nature, the memory of having done so in the past is enough to re-create many of the sensations we originally experienced. Places we connect with in a special way, when recalled, are potent suggestions for mental, emotional, and spiritual relaxation.

I have many such places, but three come to mind immediately: sitting on the cliff at the Rock of Gibraltar, I can see the Atlantic Ocean, the Straits of Gibraltar, the Mediterranean Sea, and Africa, as the history of humankind spills out in my imagination; sitting in the Andes playing my Peruvian flute while looking down at Machu Picchu, a stunning emerald green mountain peninsula surrounded on three sides by thousands of feet of air layered in early morning mist; sitting on a cliff near my childhood home where I can see the Golden Gate Bridge, the Pacific Ocean, and currents swirling around the bridge towers and racing into the San Francisco Bay.

When I want to calm myself in meditation, I imagine my

favorite spot of all . . . sitting under an oak tree in a wheat-colored field filled with purple wildflowers on the west side of Mount Tamalpais above the Pacific Ocean. Physically, I have been there dozens of times, and mentally, perhaps hundreds. I can experience the serenity of my special place no matter where I am by sitting quietly and breathing a few long, deep breaths while slowly counting backward from five, holding the image in my mind and heart.

The ability to relax depends far more on your state of mind than the location of your body. It is a gift from nature that we can use our imaginations to manage our daily lives. "Feelings are chemical and can kill or cure," says Bernie Siegel, M.D., author of *Love, Medicine and Miracles*. One of the best techniques for managing stress is to create a special place in your mind and visit it often, taking brief meditation breaks throughout the day to fully experience it. Two other exercises for learning deep feelings of physical and mental relaxation are also offered here. When all three techniques are used together, you will not only enjoy mediation time, but will have powerful strategies for staying healthy, flexible, and centered.

How to do a Special Place to Relax

Part One: Be in your special place.

Either recall a special place, or invent one in your imagination. The location of the place doesn't matter, the only requirements are that you can feel safe, relaxed, and undisturbed there. It could just as easily be a small spartan cave in the mountains as an expansive, beautiful spot on the beach. It can even be a fantasy place in another world.

Close your eyes, take three deep breaths, and allow tension to fall from your body each time you exhale. Continue to notice your breathing, counting backward from ten to one. Imagine you are approaching your place . . . walking a path, driving along a winding country road, floating into it. Whatever seems appropriate. Now you are there. What does it smell like? Do you hear birds? Is the sun warm on your face? Is the grass soft and moist with dew? Are you alone? Call as many details as possible to the scene, and lose yourself in it for a few minutes. When you are ready to leave your special place, return by the same path and count from three to one. When you reach the number one, open your eyes, stretch, and smile. You are ready to resume your activities. This exercise, when practiced regularly, grows more potent.

Part Two: The corpse pose.

In brief, you will lie on the floor and do nothing. Ironically, this is considered one of the most challenging postures in hatha yoga. Doing it properly means that your muscles must become totally relaxed, tension-free, and limp. This exercise takes you to yet another level of deep relaxation. *It only works if you do it*, so read about it, then get down on the floor and do it. One more suggestion. The next time you are feeling really mellow and stress-free, do it again. There's a very good chance you'll discover where you habitually store stress in your body even when you are in a so-called relaxed state of mind.

1. Lie on your back, your arms a few inches from your body, palms up, legs spread comfortably apart.
2. Let the floor hold your body; trust it.
3. Relax all muscles.
4. Breathe into your belly, causing your abdomen to rise and fall.

   With your eyes closed, listen to your body, being aware

of any tension you detect in your muscles. Trust the process as you scan your body with your awareness. Inhale deeply and tighten all of the muscles that feel tense. Slowly exhaling, mentally say to your muscles, "Let go. Relax." Continue scanning, tightening as you inhale, releasing as you exhale, until you have gone as far as you can go. If you wish, mentally enter your special place and enjoy a few minutes more of relaxation.

Part Three: Progressive relaxation.

Like the other two exercises, this exercise is also intended to produce a relaxation response physically and mentally. However, instead of being aware of your entire body all at once as the corpse pose suggests, this one starts at your feet and ends at your head. It takes a little more time, but is well worth it. *The process for each body part includes five steps, as follows:* (1) Begin by focusing your awareness on a single part of the body. (2) Move it around a bit, then (3) tense your muscles in that body part, pressing or contracting as intensely as possible as you inhale deeply. (4) On a quick exhale, let the tension go. (5) Release, and relax that particular body part. The shorthand for the process is:

1. focus awareness
2. movement
3. inhale and tense
4. exhale and let go
5. release and relax

Take plenty of time, starting with your toes and move slowly up your body. Do each part by itself—first the right foot, then the left. Right ankle, left ankle. Right calf, left calf, and so on. You may become aware of a tingling sensation as you "treat" each body part. This is normal. When you reach your head, be sure to include your mouth, eyes, eyelids, forehead, and scalp. Once you've completed the process, in this new state of relaxation, imagine clear, swirling energy moving up freely from your toes, throughout your entire body, and let it go out of the top of your head. Give yourself the positive suggestion that this state of relaxation is both restful and healthy. Repeat it as often as you need.

You may use this shorter two-step version to feel relaxed and invigorated almost immediately. *Step one:* Lying on ground, inhale; contract and straighten the muscles in your arms and legs while lifting them off the floor two inches. Make tight fists and tighten face muscles. Hold for three breaths. *Step two:* Exhale quickly and release the contraction. Drop your arms and legs, and breathe long and deep.

> *You can feel very happy while practicing breathing*
> *and smiling.* —Thich Nhat Hanh

Exercise 47. Volunteer
Monster: Give and Take

Ninety-nine times out of a hundred, the benefits to volunteering outweigh the effort. I do it because I get so much out of it. If you are a frequent volunteer, you already know exactly what I'm referring to. I've put in hundreds of hours supervising volunteers and being one myself in community-based programs for everything from heart disease, diabetes, conflict resolution, and education to athletics and fitness, ropes course leadership, mental health, and prison release. Most of the time I am able to offer my expertise in adventuring and risk taking, but it is the connections with people that turn me on the most about volunteering.

Ricki, a schizophrenic patient at Earth House, couldn't walk and talk at the same time when I first met her. Through ten torturous years in mental institutions, she was obsessed with self-mutilation; she ate her wrist down to the bone, smashed her hand through a plate glass window and in circling motions, ripping her arm on the jagged edge. She once placed her hand on a heater until it stuck there. Many shock treatments later, she came to Earth House, possibly her last resort before a lobotomy. Each time I went to Earth House to lead the patients on Earth Adventures, I encouraged her to look in the mirror and practice smiling. Somewhat miraculously, over time she responded to the Earth House approach and eventually recovered. She even wrote a book about it. She is now a nurse and the mother of three children. After her recovery, she told me that I gave her back her smile. She gave me something just as essential. From knowing her, I realized I needed to raise my expectations: If she could recover, perhaps anyone could.

In California, without any sort of intervention, 80 percent of released convicts return to prison. The Northern California Service League in San Francisco is a nonprofit organization that works in cooperation with the state's prison system, offering ready-for-release convicts a program called Life Skills. The people who go through the program learn about breaking old patterns, managing the peer pressure of the streets, increasing their self-esteem, and steering clear of drug and alcohol abuse, as well as basic survival essentials such as writing résumés, going on job interviews, and keeping a job once they are employed. They face huge risks as they try to put their lives back together. As a member of the Life Skills team, several times a month I spend a half day with thirty or so inmates, both men and women, exploring what it means to *Hug the Mon-*

ster and looking at ways they can take positive risks instead of the negative ones they know so well. Thanks to the program, 65 percent of the people we work with get jobs. The interactions, feedback, and results help keep me high on life.

The beauty of volunteering comes with exposure to social issues that challenge our tunnel vision, break our stereotypes, and send us heart-first into the inescapable reality of how interconnected we are. It magnifies the richness of community and offers us the chance to give something back, knowing full well we are the ones who will benefit the most. In this sense, volunteering for anything can enlarge our sense of self, deepen our capacity for compassion, and heighten the meaning and purpose of our lives.

Perhaps we'll never end all of the suffering in the world, but addressing it is good medicine. Intellectually, we may know that when we give, we always receive. But until we know it from firsthand experience, those are just nice words.

How to do Volunteer

Part One: A personal assistant.

Our lives are complicated and busy. Give yourself away for a day and offer to be someone's personal assistant. Do the grocery shopping, fix the dinner, pick up the dry cleaning, weed the flower beds, mow the lawn, wash the windows, do the Christmas wrapping, be the baby-sitter. Or type the proposal, stuff the envelopes, tidy the office, file the papers, pack and store the books.

For birthday and holiday gift giving, instead of running to the mall for a present, make clever certificates or coupon books that can be redeemed for a variety of tasks you'd be willing to do. If you'd love to receive such a gift, be the first one in your circle to offer it. You may even create a personal assistant volunteer pool so there's always a safety net of support for everyone in your immediate circle of family and friends.

Part Two: Lost horizons.

What do you want to learn more about? Most community programs that need volunteers have orientation and training programs. Expand your own repertoire of skills and your base of knowledge by spending time with an organization that will teach you something new. Or volunteer for a job you don't normally do. Step out of your professional training boundaries. If you spend time in an office all day, volunteer for some manual labor, for example. Don't have kids of your own? Become a day-camp counselor. Cook or serve Thanksgiving dinner at community shelters instead of just dropping coins in the collection basket. You can make the world a better place and be a more well-rounded person at the same time.

Part Three: "How can I help?"

If there is a special cause that is near and dear to your heart, make a commitment to become more involved instead of just sending in your annual donation. Dedicate a full year of your life to working with the organization, charity, or cause that means the most to you. If you don't have a favorite, go to your community's volunteer center and explore the many worthwhile activities that capture your imagination and your heart, with the goal of choosing one to align yourself with. Do what you love with total abandon and see what happens.

> *Let the beauty we love be what we do. There are a hundred ways to kneel and kiss the ground.*   —Rumi

Exercise 48. Be a Kid Again
Monster: Innocence

You are younger than I because you play. I stopped playing when I was a boy," confessed the dignified Nubian
crocodile hunter, smiling as he passed me a cup of tea on
the east bank of the Nile River in the Sudan. I had been
rolling down the sand dunes, running into the river, and
swimming.

Adorned in colorful beads and bright red calico fabric
wrapped from his chest to his knees, Robert (his Christian
name), twenty-nine, a Samburu warrior, told me, "You are
too young to be so old," after we had run together around
Nebor Keju in Kenya. I laughed and went off to play a game
of Frisbee with the kids in a nearby village. I was forty.

I want to die young and healthy at a great old age. To
live right up to the moment we die—now there's a goal
worth pursuing. How can we do it? Of course we must
take care of our bodies, but we must also tend to our spirits, remain open in our hearts, stimulate our minds with
new questions, stoke our curiosity with new experiences,
surround ourselves with as much love as possible, and
most of all, *play.*

Psychoschlerosis—hardening of the mind—can happen
at any age. As celebrations, birthdays are great. As rites of
passage, certain birthdays have more meaning than others.
But chronological age doesn't mean all that much in the big
picture. The reminder to "act our age" is not good advice
most of the time. Perhaps one of the important tasks of
adulthood is to cultivate the magic of childhood. To lose
ourselves to the joy of a day and fall into bed at night, exhausted and satisfied—this is the fine art of living a full life.
If we look, act, and feel younger than our chronological

age, we're doing something very right. It probably means we've discarded a lot of social programming and rejected the notion that getting older means having less fun.

Even if you don't have fond memories of your own life as a kid, as someone wisely observed, "It is never to late to have a happy childhood." Being a kid again doesn't mean we should dwell in the past. Remembering how, long ago, we played hide and seek with our pals isn't the same thing as *playing hide and seek right now*. And it is the *right now* quality of life where the kid can be found in you. It is about discovering our innocence, letting go of judgments, and being an enthusiastic participant in life.

How to do Be a Kid Again

Part One: Lighten up.

Ask yourself these questions. Who is the youngest person in spirit you know? How old is that person? How old are you? How old are you in spirit? Who are your role models for aging? How do you feel toward people who appear to take life lightly? On a scale of one to ten, with one being serious and ten being lighthearted, where would you rate yourself? If you are a ten, you'll be eager to dive in to Part Two of this exercise. If you rate yourself a five or less, do not pass Go. Proceed straight to a playground, the zoo, or if you are really serious-minded, the children's section of your local library, and rediscover the magic of childhood play.

Part Two: Play.

Do as many of the following activities in the coming month as you can. Roll down a hill. Skip rope. Play hopscotch. Do a cartwheel. Go barefoot. Finger paint. Get some crayons and a coloring book, and don't stay within the lines. Blow bubbles. Find a mud puddle and land in it with both feet. Ride your bike in the rain. Watch Saturday morning cartoons in your pj's with a bowl of your favorite cereal. Buy a stuffed animal and cuddle with it at night. Play with dolls. Be the biggest kid at the children's museum. Get some comic books. Play silly tricks on people at work. Pass out bubble gum and have a contest to see who can cover his or her face with the biggest pink glob. Giggle. Organize a game of kickball, hide and seek, sandlot baseball, red light/green light, Mother may I?, or kick the can. Sit in a sandbox and build castles. Buy a Frisbee for everyone you know. Tour a toy store and come home with Erector sets, Lincoln Logs, and games for everyone in the house. Sit on Santa's lap. Color Easter eggs. Make valentines. At your next birthday party, play musical chairs, pin the tail on the donkey, and wear silly hats. Put the number of candles on the cake that represent how old you feel, not how old you are.

> *We are all born charming, fresh, and spontaneous and*
> *must be civilized before we are fit to participate in society.*
> —Miss Manners (Judith Martin)

Exercise 49. In Silence
Monster: Inner Awareness

In 1995 I made my second trip to India to do research for a work of fiction, and to have some new adventures along the Ganges River in the Himalayas. Among the places Sandy and I visited was an amazingly beautiful ashram in Poona. Thousands of spiritual seekers from all over the world, mostly from highly developed, westernized cultures, visit this ashram. Some, like us, stay for a few days. Others stay for weeks, months, even years working on various aspects of themselves. Classes are offered in everything from meditation and Zen archery to art, theater, and dance. It was fairly common to see people wearing a small white button that said "In Silence," indicating to others that the individual was practicing the discipline of silence and was not available for conversation or even eye contact. The length of time a person is in silence varies from a few days to a few weeks. The discipline is intended to draw the consciousness completely inward.

Of course, the practice isn't new. In most major religions, certain orders of priests, nuns, and monks have been doing it for centuries. But observing "nonreligious" people adopting it as a method of inner awareness was impressive. They struck me as being particularly courageous folks who were actively engaged in hugging monsters.

Susan RoAne, author of the best-selling book *How to Work a Room*, is a friend of mine. As a writer and public speaker specializing in the ways people network and communicate, she has magnificent expertise in the art of conversation. Ironically, when she developed polyps on her vocal chords, her medical treatment included not talking for one entire month. Being silent for a full month as someone who earns her living as an expert in conversation and communication was, according to her, profoundly instructive.

Making changes in our lives gets easier as we pay closer attention to our responses to a variety of stimuli in the environment. Habitual responses may be an indication that we aren't as awake, aware, and connected as we could be. They can block us from being fully present to see, listen, and experience the more subtle and sublime qualities of life around us. By maintaining silence, we get to notice familiar behavior patterns and realize that we are capable of changing them. In those moments of discovery and perhaps revelation, we are more free.

How to do In Silence

Part One: For beginners.

My own wilderness adventures have taught me plenty about the virtues and rewards of silence. If you've never had the experience, you are in for a real treat. You may be interested in doing this exercise for spiritual reasons. Perhaps you are a compulsive talker who really needs to learn how to be still. Or, maybe you just waste too much time talking on the phone. Whatever your motivation, consider yourself in training for this exercise, and develop your endurance in increments.

Begin with a clear intention to be in silence. Mark off a fifteen-minute period and be conscious about not speaking. Be fully present, going about your normal activities, but don't talk. Practice this fifteen-minute exercise each day for one week. Then, gradually extend the amount of time in fifteen-minute increments. You'll discover new ways to communicate with people by writing notes, using facial expressions, and gesturing with your hands. If you are going to try this at work, inform your colleagues so you'll have their support. Make your own little button to wear, or hang a sign on your office door to make it easier for everyone.

Part Two: For advanced beginners.

The more advanced level of this exercise is to declare a full day of silence for yourself, and to observe it regularly,

such as the last Saturday of each month or every Wednesday, selecting a frequency that suits your lifestyle. How you
spend that day depends upon the monster you are hugging. You may need to declare it as a spiritual retreat where
you set aside all other activities but those of reflection and
meditation. If so, consider eating only fruit on that day, letting your body rest and cleanse itself. Simply taking a vacation from the demands of the telephone and idle conversation is good use of this, too. Regardless of how you
approach it, your inner awareness will be heightened. If
you discover you really enjoy being in silence, consider
going on a weekend, weeklong, or even monthlong retreat
where the retreat environment totally supports your intention. When you return to speaking, you'll discover a mindfulness of detail and an awareness of yourself that wasn't
there before.

> *I have three entire days alone—three pure and*
> *rounded pearls.*   —Virginia Woolf

Exercise 50. Imagine
Monster: The Future

There's a spot in New York City's Central Park with an inspiring mosaic mandala placed at a juncture in the walk-
ways that wind through lovely gardens known as Straw-
berry Fields. Donated by Yoko Ono in memory of John
Lennon, the mandala features a sunburst-type design. In
the center, expressed in charcoal-colored tiles, is the simple
declaration, "Imagine." The gardens are filled with some

of the world's endangered flowers, plants, and trees. A gentle place that easily invites a contemplative state of mind, it is an elegant, fitting shrine to both the unthinkable and the possible . . . and all of the variations in between.

Imagination is the first step of any creative act, and as such, it can sometimes have a mystical or spiritual quality to it. I have mentioned elsewhere in *Hug the Monster* a series of events I performed in 1972 called Everyman's Olympics, an Adventure Decathlon. The idea for it actually came to me fully formed in a meditation, in which I saw myself performing ten different events, each one in a different location in Europe and Africa. Although the final "real-life version" was slightly different than that which I perceived in my meditation, it was essentially the same in all of the important ways. The inspiration was my response to the upcoming Munich Olympics, and what I was perceiving as a major loss of the original Olympic ideals. Pathological national pride and political agendas fueled by media hype were destroying what was once a meaningful celebration of human athletic achievement. I must have tuned in to something in the air, because eventually, as you may recall, blood was shed at the Munich Olympics and people were killed.

To the extent that the future is unknown, it is the land of adventure, opportunity, and the thrilling prospect that our dreams may be coming true . . . somewhere out there. To be sure, there are times in our lives when the future is more known and secure. During these times we can coast a little bit, perhaps taking a well-deserved rest after a period of intense productivity, change, and/or challenge. But these periods shouldn't last long, nor should we take more rest than we need. The actions of today are seeds that will take root, grow, and begin to sprout sooner than we realize.

Knowing that we'll reap what we sow, mindfulness at all times is a good policy.

Hugging monsters keeps us in the present moment where the potential for change is greatest. But when the future invites our thoughts, we have the faculties to respond with creativity and love. We can imagine a bright future resulting from such intentions, and as we conjure up the desires of our heart, we recommit ourselves to living as fully as possible.

The technique I'm referring to is most often called visualization, but for those whose inner senses are more tuned to sound or touch, the term is often misunderstood. To visualize something means to picture it as real in your mind's eye. We can project our ideas like a mental movie onto a screen in our mind and experience them as they unfold. Some people say they can't "see" anything when they visualize, and that's only because the language falls short, not the visualizer. Depending upon your own understanding of the process, "think of the ocean" may yield the same experience as "see the ocean" or "picture the ocean" or "imagine the ocean." However, when other sensing words are introduced, the experience can be richer and more powerful. "Hear the ocean in your mind," "Feel the ocean," and "Smell the ocean" each expand the experience.

In the same way, when we visualize the future, using all of our inner senses is like fine-tuning the receiver on the radio or focusing a camera lens. Adding the detail of sensory-rich information, we sharpen our intentions. We get clearer about things. The entire experience can be enhanced even more when done in a quiet, meditative state of mind.

I've also known people who visualize the behavior changes they are working on. For example, while dieting, you may visualize your future body, seeing yourself in new clothes, standing in front of the mirror admiringly, or on the bathroom scales where the numbers register the ideal weight as an accomplished fact. You may also imagine hearing compliments, or feeling lighter as you walk up a flight of stairs. Visualization is used as a support to reach other kinds of goals. People visualize the future to see their new car, the positive outcome of a project at work, or their advanced degree.

Some people believe that visualizing in this way actually attracts the content of the images into your life. I find it an interesting theory, but how it works isn't that important to me. When we take the time to be with ourselves, we touch our own potential and gain access to parts of ourselves that we may not always be aware of. It is a very creative place where solutions to problems may emerge, where intuition seems to be enhanced, and where we can experience the ways in which we are connected to all of life.

How to do Imagine

Part One: For beginners—active visualization.

Select a goal you are working on right now. It can be anything from filing your taxes on time, selling your home, or completing a project at work, to a behavior change such as becoming a nonsmoker, a former nail-biter, or a person at his or her ideal state of health and fitness. Next, ask yourself the following questions. How much time will it reasonably take to reach the goal? What are the necessary steps required? What resources are needed? What are the missing pieces in order for the event or goal to be completed to your satisfaction and with the highest good for all concerned? Once you've established all of the facts, close your eyes and visualize the outcome. Put yourself in the future where the event is an accomplished fact. See the date on the calendar, for example. Fill in as many details as possible and experience them with your inner senses of hearing, seeing, smelling, tasting, and touching. Repeat this process regularly, such as each evening before you fall asleep, or every morning before you get out of bed. It only takes a few minutes. You can also recall the images anytime throughout the day.

Part Two: Passive visualization.

For this exercise, select a problem or situation in which the outcome or solution isn't yet clear to you. Using the same process of engaging your inner sensing faculties, examine the situation, mulling over various possible outcomes. Play a variety of scenarios in your mind while holding the question, "What is best for me and all concerned?" Remain open to new ideas by being in your heart as well as your head. The effectiveness of the exercise will increase if you take time to meditate first, clearing your mind and body of stress, tension, and noise.

This is called passive visualization because you are not yet in the goal-achievement mode where the outcome is already very obvious. In Part One, you simply strengthen your commitment to what is known. In Part Two, you acknowledge openness for insights, ideas, and help. This openness will make it possible for you to be more objective, reduce tunnel vision, and set the ego aside so that the best possible solution has a greater chance of coming to you.

> *Whatever you can do or dream you can do, begin it. Boldness has genius, power, and magic to it.* —Geothe

Exercise 51. *Play Dead*
Monster: Lack of Meaning and Purpose

I have faced my death a number of times, and never on purpose. In Kenya, I was once camping in the bush near a water hole when strange shuffling noises woke me up. Exhausted from a strenuous day of adventure running, I wondered if the sounds came from my imagination. Then they grew louder. My mind raced through the possibilities, the sounds intensifying. I wondered if the Shifta, a notorious group of poachers and bandits, armed with automatic weapons, were getting ready to attack us. Why would they make so much noise? I wondered. Due to a local hunting ban, they would know we weren't armed.

My fear catapulted me into action, as an electrified, euphoric state of energy took over. *I refused to die in my sleeping bag.* I slipped into my running shoes, unzipped my tent, and stared in total disbelief at the approaching huge dark shapes—a herd of elephants heading straight for our camp. Their trumpeting split the night as about eighty of them stampeded, trampling and huffing through the campsite. Amazingly, no one was killed or even hurt.

Reflecting on life and death was an automatic response in this instance once the crisis had passed. I have used the memory of this experience on any number of occasions when I've needed to check in with myself on how my life is going. Great insights come from the brink because when consciousness is heightened, energy flows. From this flowing comes the awesome experience of being fully alive.

On a more humorous note, when I was a kid I carried a folded piece of paper in my pocket to convey a message to whoever found me on the chance I would be killed on my way to a bomb shelter. In those days government propaganda stirred up all kinds of fears that the bad guys—communists—would drop a bomb any minute. The note, intended for my tombstone, read: "I love ice hockey. David Miln Smith."

All great myths carry the theme of death and rebirth. And throughout history, spiritual leaders and inner explorers have reported the importance of facing our mortality as a gateway or entry point to leading a fulfilling life. Ironically, to face the reality that *one day we will absolutely die* is to be able to live with less fear and more joy. It is as if once our limitations as humans are honestly acknowledged, we are freer to make the most of whatever life brings us. Many of us who have experienced the death of a loved one already understand the monumental shift in thinking that comes from facing death. Yet, you don't necessarily need to have your own near-death experience to get the wisdom of the following exercises. The central idea is simple. *Imagine today is your last day on Earth as you. How will you live it?* As George Santayana wisely said, "There is no cure for birth and death, save to enjoy the interval."

How to do Play Dead

Part One: Regrets and second chances.

Close your eyes and imagine you are about to take your final breath. Ask yourself these questions. Have you ever wondered what gift you have to give the world? Or to put it another way, how is the world a better place because you've lived? What do you regret not doing? Are there things you want to say to those close to you? Elisabeth Kubler-Ross, a physician, has written extensively about death and dying. In her experience, those who hold on the tightest and scream the loudest at death's door are those who haven't lived as fully as they could have—who have sorrowful regrets. What images and issues are triggered by visualizing your own death? How would your life be different if you practiced having this awareness regularly?

If you have a strong fear of death, begin breaking the fear down into bits and pieces. Read a few books on near-death experiences, or talk to people who have survived extreme illness or trauma. If they will share their insights with you, listen very closely, for perhaps they have been somewhere you haven't been.

Do a practice draft of your last will and testament, and write "last letters" to loved ones. Reflect on the fact that your life had a beginning, and it will have an end.

Part Two: Your obituary and tombstone.

Imagine you died today. Write your obituary by projecting into the future and then "seeing" the past in front of you. What did you accomplish? What did you enjoy the most? The least? How is the world better, different, or unchanged because you lived? What dreams went unfulfilled? What surprises come up as you imagine the end of your life? Don't just think about it. Take action. Put the words on paper. For another version of the same exercise, draft the words on your imaginary tombstone. In one line, what did your life stand for?

Part Three: If today were the final day . . .

Go through the next week with this waking thought: *If today were my last day, what would make it count the most?* Sure we are grateful for everything that makes our lives wonderful, it's just that *we often cease to experience them as real, vital, and precious once they have been stored in our memories as thoughts, ideas, and past experiences.* This isn't about a guilt trip, it is a lesson in how the brain can keep us from being present. Somehow it is easier to retrieve the memory of someone and project it from experience rather than having an encounter with that person *in the moment where new possibilities exist*. The exercise is worth doing, and gets easier with practice. For example:

What if you were seeing the faces of friends and colleagues for the last time? Or were enjoying your final cup of morning coffee . . . your last drive through the tree-lined parkway in autumn . . . your very last dinner at home. . . . You won't again see the daffodils come up in spring . . . or shiver at winter's first snow . . . or hear your daughter's voice calling you for help from the other room. . . .

Notice how, as the list of moments takes shape, it can become a virtual inventory for all of the people, places, and experiences you cherish. Done in a spirit of gratitude, this exercise can instantly open your heart and heighten awareness not about dying, but rather about living fully, completely, and without regrets.

Always stay in your own movie.   —*Ken Kesey*

Exercise 52. Open Heart
Monster: Reality

Hugging monsters is my way of loving, and of remembering where *real life* is happening all of the time. It seems like a paradox, but the spirit of adventuring—living in the unknown, inviting the new and unexpected—*leads me into love*. To put it another way, when I think *I know*, when I am 100 percent certain of anything, I am no longer open. I've shut down. The adventure is over. I've lost my connection. Staying awake, being present in the moment, is the only way to have the experience of being where love is real. *If we want to feel love, we have to be in our own light* in the same way that we must be in our bodies to feel hunger. Doing so, we realize that our light has a source. How we grasp that realization is how we live with the fathomless mystery of our own being. Ray Bradbury put it this way: "Sometimes I think I understand everything. Then I regain consciousness."

A discussion of love is a tricky thing. In the context of *Hug the Monster*, we are looking at the value and benefits of living our lives with as much openness as possible. Although it is somewhat difficult, we want to avoid intellectual examinations of love; for our purposes here, we want to focus on taking action, on love *as movement charged with the highest intentions*. How you define the differences between self-love, romantic love, friendship, love between family members, love of God, and, most broadly, love and compassion for humanity, is a matter of your own experience, culture, upbringing, and belief systems. Yet, underlying all of the ways we love, there seems to be a common energy link, a simple melody line if you will, that suggests we may be able to enjoy more love if we can get at the dynamic qualities of love, that perhaps in all of our loving experiences, the same music is there whether it takes the form of a lullaby or a symphony, a rock 'n' roll number or a sonata, a majestic hymn sung by a thousand voices or a solo gently hummed in solitude.

Love involves a spirit of openness, and of connection at the same time. The warm feelings that we associate with love have a wide range. I love my life—my partner, children, friends, work, travel, education, recreation, and on and on. We each have our lists. The contents of our lives, we say, are the things we love. Yet, on closer inspection, it isn't the contents of our lives that we love at all. They are the meeting points in which we most easily experience *loving*. As a concept, love is confusing. We stumble over distinctions between healthy self-love and generosity, or between being selfish and self-sacrificing. Often, we aspire to unconditional love, and then in reality we attach conditions, limits, and judgments. It bounces back at us, almost defying words. But as something we do, it becomes crystal clear. Love is present when we connect lovingly. Nobody can do it for us. To maintain an open heart, the monster is none other than daily reality.

When it comes to taking action, it seems there is plenty of fear associated with loving. For example, we fear being vulnerable, and sometimes our vulnerability causes us to withdraw or close our hearts. Protecting ourselves, we *want* to hug the monster, but find, to our disappointment, that we can only offer a handshake instead. Remembering it is okay to feel vulnerable, we must learn how to maintain the connection with whatever is generating the fearful feelings. Eventually, when we are ready, an insight will occur, or our awareness will expand and we will be able to hug the vulnerability monster.

Other love-related fears seem to work in a similar way. The dynamic is paradoxical. To connect, we have to let go. Until we stop holding on, we can't love. "Love is letting go of fear," wrote Gerald Jampolsky, M.D., in a little book by the same name. *Love* is word loaded with baggage and filled with assumptions, perhaps because it is the one feeling that we assume we all share. But our personalities are complex and varied. As an expectation or a goal, love is most often associated with pleasure, desire, security, trust, and disappointment. Let's see if we can unpack those bags a bit. . . .

How can we grasp the meaning of an open heart and come into love freely? We can easily agree that the world would be a better place with more love in it. We can sense the love of those close to us—family and friends. We can say we love our spouse and children, our work, tennis, pizza, and a good book. But what do all of these objects of love have in common? A book is just so many words on a page; the light of comprehension comes from you. A pizza is just dough, sauce, and toppings. The pleasure of eating is not contained in the pizza. It is in you. *Name anything or anyone that you love, and notice it is you who has the light, you who moves into love.*

"There are two parallel tasks in spiritual life. One is to discover selflessness, the other is to develop a healthy sense of self. Both sides of that apparent paradox must be fulfilled for us to awaken," writes Jack Kornfield in his wonderful book, *A Path with Heart: The Perils and Promises of Spiritual Life.*

If we think love indicates the absence of pain and suffering, we have attached ourselves to an idea and we miss the mark. Being present at someone's death, there is no question that love is real, and that it exists beyond, or in spite of, any particular emotional state. From soothing a child's injured knee, to listening to a friend unload about an awful day, to rescuing a frightened puppy, to noticing all of the injustice in the world . . . we can learn to be with all of life's experiences, and still be in love. If we see love only as an emotion, we are living in a very limited reality. Emotions are like waves. They wash over us, but rarely do they change us. Love, on the other hand, not only changes us, it transforms us.

How to do Open Heart

Part One: Invite love.

Inviting love to be present in our lives goes beyond a positive mental attitude. It is an orientation, an awareness, a state of being. So don't think about love. Don't analyze what it is, isn't, or might be. For this exercise, just be aware of everything and everyone you love while doing the following meditation, a metaphor for opening your heart. As you do so, pay special attention to the incredible lack of judgments in an open heart, and how fully accepting you are of who and what you love. As a meditation, be sure to spend a few minutes breathing and relaxing before beginning the visualization below.

Imagine your heart as a single rosebud. Picturing it vividly, let each velvety-soft petal represent the awareness of more love as you allow the rosebud to slowly open and blossom fully. Begin by recalling familiar faces. Stay with those images as long as you wish. Next, begin to add those faces, images, and situations in which you would be willing to feel love. Play them like mental movies if that helps you focus. In other words, include the things and people in your world that you haven't yet associated with loving feelings, such as people at work or strangers at the post office. Begin making those associations. See how big you can make the rose, and how open your heart can be, gradually adding more and more images.

Here's the leap: Actively imagine the personal benefits of being able to look at the entire world and your total life experience in the same way.

Part Two: Express love without words.

Can you consider the possibility that everything in life is exactly perfect just as it is? Or, to put it another way, that it is the unknown outcome and not the "facts" that contain opportunities to move into love? What kinds of events or interactions diminish loving feelings in your days? How about some of these: You are stuck in traffic, twenty minutes late for your next appointment. The copy machine is down and you feel like blaming the secretary for the fact that important papers won't be duplicated in time for the monthly staff meeting. You are in the middle of a heated argument with your spouse. The baby-sitter just canceled for the third time in a row. Your best friend is moving two thousand miles away. Can you imagine holding your heart wide open throughout any of these common scenarios?

Here's the exercise. Explore unconditional love as an experience. Without using words, for one entire ordinary day, make being in love with life your only intention. Discover and notice the ways in which this comes easily, and the ways in which you hesitate, or cut yourself off from moving into love. Don't plan it or anticipate your actions and reactions. Let love move and carry you throughout the day like the gentle currents of a friendly river. Let your responses be spontaneous, loving, and open. Accept, feel, and experience everything that comes up. See if it is possible to have all of the elements of an ordinary day, including frustrations, anger, challenges, and still be in a place where love is real. Be a student and let love be your teacher.

Learn to wish that everything should come to
pass exactly as it does. —Epictetus

Chapter Eight

Conclusion
Pomp and Circumstance

*Life's fulfillment finds constant contradictions in its path,
but those are necessary for the sake of its advance.*
—Rabindranath Tagore

On each new adventure, the thrills, challenges, successes, and failures of previous adventures travel with me. The spirits of those I have loved are constant companions in my memory, and the most valuable lessons of experience find new applications in new challenges. I am passionate about hugging monsters as a way of life. In *Illusions*, by Richard Bach, we are given the following clear advice. "Here is a test to find out if your mission on Earth is finished. If you are alive, it isn't." And so, we must keep going. . . .

Halfway over Mount Tamalpais while participating in the rugged fourteen-mile Double Dipsea Run, my seven-year-old daughter, Chelsea, was really struggling to keep up. An attitude started to form. She stopped, put her hands defiantly on her hips, and declared with straight-faced insistence, "Daddy, I want a helicopter and I want it right now!" And while, of course, there was no helicopter to rescue her from the challenge, her sentiment was a poignant reminder of how it is in life. When we've had enough, we just want out. Good for her for being so clear about her needs. And good for her that once her needs were declared, she was able to go on to become the youngest person ever to finish the Double Dipsea run.

Sometimes in hugging monsters, so much stuff comes up that we need to take a break, sit down, and catch our breath. And when those moments come, that's exactly what we *should* do.

Changes *happen* in life. Sometimes we choose the monsters, and other times they choose us. But when we hug them, courageously stepping into the unknown, we make precious memories that gird our resolve and fuel our growth.

Sandy writes of the ending of an old life and the beginning of her new one:

> I was just about finished packing boxes in the living room and saying final good-byes to my big house in the Indianapolis suburbs. I was sad, exhausted, and terrified. I assaulted myself with the questions one more time. Was I nuts? Getting a divorce seemed like the right move for me, but leaving my family, friends, and lifetime roots and moving three thousand miles away where I didn't know a single person, how could this be a great idea? What if it didn't work out? What if I couldn't earn a living and support myself? What if I hated it out there in California? Drowning in wads of newspaper and packing tape, I seriously considered calling it all off. "It's not too late to change your mind, you know," I reminded myself.
>
> A little voice inside responded, "You invented this dream, Sandy. If you don't put yourself out there, you'll never know how things might have been. *Can you live with a regret that big?*" Tears spilled down my face, dripping onto the framed lithograph on my lap, half-wrapped. The radio, tuned to my favorite classical station, offered a musical punch line to my dilemma as the opening strains of the traditional graduation march, "Pomp and Circumstance," filled the moment. Simultane-

ously, framed through the big picture window, I looked
up to see my Mayflower moving van slowly, in synch
with the music, pulling into place in front of my house.
It was the end of a movie with an unforgettable sound
track. I groaned, then laughed through my tears. It was
all too perfect. Literally, graduation day was here. I took
my final cues from a benevolent universe that clearly had
a sense of humor, and never looked back.

We graduate more than once or twice in a lifetime. If
we're lucky, it happens again and again as the cycles of life
carry, lead, or push us out there into the world. We gather
our experiences, apply our hard-earned skills, and test our
knowledge in new settings, saying good-bye to classmates
and teachers at each and every turning point. At the inter-
sections where the known world meets the unknown territory, the only thing we can be certain of is that new monsters
are waiting for us. It is perhaps nature's creative way of
working on herself.

So Long, Monsters?

Are the monsters ever gone for good? I suspect the answer is "no" if you are committed to living in the light of
your full potential. I know someone who proudly offers
that she has read Scott Peck's classic, *The Road Less Traveled*,
six times. "I read it, work on myself, discover new questions, and read it again. There is always more to do," she
explains. I admire that.

Hug the Monster is a philosophy for living, not a pre-
scription for life. The exercises are not scientific, and there
are thousands of possible variations. You won't find black
and white answers to your most essential questions anywhere in the text. At best it is a handy compass, not a map.

This is quite on purpose. Our lives can't be quantified to a standard measurement. Anyone who claims to know all of the answers is advertising their ignorance. Or as someone wisely observed, "If you meet the Buddha on the road, shoot him."

We trust that you found some motivation, a little courage, a playful spirit, and a confirmation that yes, life is difficult, and yes, it is worth every ounce of joy, pain, and frustration it gives us. As an antidote for feelings of isolation and confusion, a friendly voice to cheer you on in your progress, or your own private coach to offer training, guidance, and workout suggestions, *Hug the Monster* is, hopefully, a book you will return to often. In life, we can never have too many reminders to *take action*, to get out of our heads, where the fear is, and into our hearts, where we can embrace the things that immobilize us. And now that you have learned a five-step method for overcoming obstacles and taking action, you have a reliable approach where perhaps before you were less systematic or focused.

Self-Mastery or Healing?

What is human nature? Is there such a thing as self-mastery, and if so, what does the end result look like? What exactly can we control, and what are we powerless to do anything about when it comes to our own lives? As humans, we are curious beings, yet we cannot deny that, biologically and spiritually, we are part of the natural world where everywhere a mysterious message suggests we are participants in a self-correcting, self-healing system. Everything seems bent on creation, destruction, and creation again. Our tragedies can become our blessings, our failures can blossom to become our victories. If we attend to the process, perhaps the creation becomes more magnificent with each go around. If so, then hugging monsters, affirming what is real and what is not, is an integral part of the process of healing. It is our contribution to the creation, and it would seem that we are responsible for doing our part. No one else's life looks exactly like yours or mine. We can only puzzle over or offer conjecture as to someone else's role in the big scheme of things. But we can, with diligence, discover and perform our own job with greater awareness, art, and skill.

Change, inherent in the natural order of things, is only the territory. Fear is nature's way of clearing a path, of saying, "Wake up. Pay attention. Go *this* way, not *that* way." Growth is our response to the directive. I am fairly certain that we choose the timing of our growth, because no matter what is going on, we can learn to alter our responses. Accept it now, or put it off until another time, but eventually we will have to do the work required of us. At least that's how it all makes sense to me.

Have you noticed there is something in our nature that enjoys a good fright? Millions of us love horror films and cliff-hangers filled with danger. As kids, we sat around campfires telling each other ghost stories so we could experience the rush of the fear in our imaginations. "The scariest thing for me is the shower scene in the Hitchcock movie *Psycho.* I've seen it twenty times," commented someone when asked to name her biggest fears. We go to theme parks and ride bigger, scarier, gravity-defying roller-coasters to deliver a thrilling shock to our systems. Children enjoy twirling around and around for the delicious sensation of dizziness, and falling back onto the ground to feel the Earth spinning beneath them. When Chelsea was was so young she was barely able to talk, she constantly begged, "Chase me, Daddy!" Sufi dancing, known as whirling, is actually finding a resurgence in the popular culture as a form of moving meditation. I recently heard it is offered as part of a mind/body fitness program in an athletic club on the East Coast.

Perhaps it is natural to put ourselves off balance, and to enjoy fear for the sheer exhilaration of it, as well as the feeling of safety once we are calm and centered again. In this way, perhaps hugging monsters is organic. In order to find our center, we must spin to the outer edge of our own orbits from time to time. If this is nature's gift to us, then hugging monsters is an apt metaphor for an experience that is our birthright and our obligation.

So, congratulations. If you've made it this far, you have found something of yourself in these pages. Maybe the flash of recognition was instant in many of the exercises. Perhaps you found only a few that were authentically difficult. But you aren't off the hook just yet. Here are some final questions for you to answer. Which exercises did you gravitate to most easily and naturally? Why? Which ones did you skip altogether? Why? Can you imagine going back to do them at another time? And which ones worked really well for you? What results did they produce?

How Uncomfortable Did You Get?

Our comfort zones get tested when we hug monsters. In fact, an important sign of growth is a feeling of discomfort. It is natural and normal. Perhaps new levels of intensity surfaced as you expanded yourself. If you found yourself moving between excitement and depression, for example, as the exercises pushed your limits or your buttons, maybe you had to set the book aside for a while. If this was your experience, hopefully you also realized that the difficult exercises can be saved and worked on another time, and that you can continue learning with those that felt easier or safer. Always grant yourself permission to grow at a rate that is only slightly uncomfortable, and not overwhelming. Take your time, and steady your resolve.

What category of monsters seemed most relevant to your life? Perhaps you found the Eternal Monsters most difficult, or maybe many of the Relationship Monsters were the easiest. If you followed the cross-training metaphor, you created a balanced program of monster hugging and selected exercises from each category as a set to be worked on. Did you use the buddy system for added support? Did you honestly go handle a snake, give a speech in public, and write your epitaph? Can you enjoy going to work a new way now even though it means a longer trip? Are you healthier and more fit? Did you find your LifeSport? How about this time next year, will you keep it up? Did you get some unwanted habits under control? Are your troubled relationships in better shape? Can you jump like a Samburu warrior or scrunch your face up and roar like a lion? Have you integrated meditation into your life? Did you play like a kid? Have you completed your home video yet? Are you having more fun?

Commencement Day Is Here

If you feel more connected to yourself, to others, and to the world, you've accomplished a great deal. Don't stop now. Take another look at the dreams and fears you wrote down at the beginning of the warm-up exercises. Target a few new ones and begin again. Our lives are a work in progress, and who can say when we will be finished? For every graduation, there is a commencement. As long as there are monsters to hug, there is plenty to be done. From this day forward and for all of your life, may you find the courage to hug every monster, and may every monster hug you back.

One final note. Our Monster Hugging Hall of Fame is waiting to be filled with your success stories. While I was writing this summary, a friend who has been reading the manuscript and offering her experience with the exercises as feedback phoned from her office. "I'm a black cat today. It's Halloween and I decided to dress up, thanks in part to *Hug the Monster*." Normally a more reserved person, she was energized and laughing as she made her report. Thanks, Violet. And *way to go*.

As you work with the exercises in *Hug the Monster*, if you have meaningful experiences, we really want to know about them. Tell us how a particular exercise inspired you to take action. We'd also enjoy learning about new exercises, tips, and helpful hints you may invent or hear about that involve hugging monsters and making changes in our lives with less fear and more joy. Please write to us at with your feedback: Hug the Monster, P.O. Box 3240, Santa Cruz, CA 95063 3240. Or you may e-mail your stories and comments to MonsterHug@aol.com. Thanks.

Things do not change. We change.
  —Henry David Thoreau

Index of Exercises

About the Authors

David Miln Smith is an American original with a résumé that defies convention. As a world-class adventurer, for over three decades his quest has been to discover, experience, and embrace the highest and best of the human spirit. His career credits include kayaking two thousand miles down the Nile, trekking the Sahara solo, and being the first man to swim from Africa to Europe. In addition, he created the events for NBC's *Survival of the Fittest* competition and has been on the cover of *Sports Illustrated* as a pioneering athlete who expanded sports beyond traditional team competitions and into new categories of fun, fitness, and personal challenge.

His creative life has required that he become an expert on health and fitness, risk taking, world travel, outdoor adventure, team building, and making friends. Because he exemplifies his own can-do message, his work as a motivational speaker, writer, frequent talk-show guest, and adventure guide has inspired thousands of people to embrace their fears and get more out of life. He is the author of two other books, *The East-West Exercise Book* and *Healing Journey: The Odyssey of an Uncommon Athlete*. A native of San Francisco and father of two teenagers, he lives in Santa Cruz, California. He holds a Ph.D. in health and human services.

Sandra Leicester is vice president of Guerrilla Marketing International, a California-based company that helps businesspeople market their companies and themselves more creatively. She is a former advertising agency executive and for ten years ran her own public-relations and marketing company. A lifelong student of human potential, psychology, and spirituality, at midcareer she radically changed directions in order to test her self-knowledge and pursue new dreams. She now draws upon all of those experiences in her work as a writer, marketing guru, and inspirational speaker. A native of Indianapolis, Indiana, she lives in Santa Cruz, California.